To Lynn

Be fearlessly authentic!
Keep being awesome
mama!
— Laura Duds

This Caffeinated Life

SURVIVING MOTHERHOOD WITH HUMOR, SARCASM, GRIT, GRACE, GOD, AND A LOT OF CAFFEINE

LAURA DEEDS

WESTBOW
PRESS®
A DIVISION OF THOMAS NELSON
& ZONDERVAN

WestBow Press books may be ordered through booksellers or by contacting:

WestBow Press
A Division of Thomas Nelson & Zondervan
1663 Liberty Drive
Bloomington, IN 47403
www.westbowpress.com
844-714-3454

Interior Image Credit: McKenna McNelly Photography

Taken from the HOLY BIBLE: EASY-TO-READ VERSION ©2014
by Bible League International. Used by permission.

ISBN: 978-1-6642-3781-0 (sc)
ISBN: 978-1-6642-3782-7 (hc)
ISBN: 978-1-6642-3779-7 (e)

Library of Congress Control Number: 2021912613

Print information available on the last page.

WestBow Press rev. date: 08/05/2021

To my grandmother, whom my talent for writing comes from, who faithfully reads my epistles, and who encourages me to keep telling my stories.

Preface

The words have not always flowed quickly or easily. Some days, I sit, with my fingers on the keyboard, and *will* them to move and type words and paragraphs that will make sense and inspire others. Yet nothing comes. There are no words, funny stories, or inspiring chapters. My fingers just lie still on the keyboard. I feel like a failure and want to quit. Doubt and fear consume the thoughts in my head. They tell me, *No one will ever want to read this.*

Then out of nowhere while I'm listening to a song and my mind is on a hundred other little things, that idea or inspiration hits me. Before it is gone from my head, I pull out my laptop, my phone voice notes, or even just the corner of today's page in my planner so that I can jot down that thought. I don't want to let it escape. There may not be another idea for a while. My head may be filled with too many worries, anxious thoughts, to-do lists, or fatigue, and then this keyboard may sit idle for some time to come.

But I still have stories to tell. I still have advice to pass along. I did it the hard way, and I want to encourage you to do it differently. I'm further down the road of life, and I can fill what feels like mundane days with humorous stories, sarcasm, and a little encouragement to get you through it. Maybe, a few insightful notes from my gram will encourage you instead. Whatever it may be, I just keep clacking away at these keys because just as I have been inspired time and time again by other moms, wives, writers, and hot messes, I hope that I can might encourage a few of them too.

I'm far from perfect—so far from it that I'm on a busy interstate going the wrong direction. I haven't washed my hair in a day and a half. I don't workout often enough. I eat too many snacks and drink too much caffeine. I don't play board games often enough with my kids, only cook dinner three times a week, and don't bake cookies from scratch. I think about work when I'm at home and think about home when I'm at work. I don't know what makes me think I can write down these thoughts and that someone will one day want to read them. Maybe no one will. But still I plug away at this machine, in a dark room and with only the keys to light what I am doing.

I guess it's therapy. Typing away and hearing the little clacks on the keyboard are soothing to me. It settles my restless soul to get out the thoughts that are bottled up inside, to write what is stirring inside me, and to say the things that I am too scared to say out loud. That is therapy. So on and on I go. Hang on!

I'm an Addict

*Y*ep, I'm tired too. Oh, you didn't actually ask if I was tired, did you? I assumed that if you had a moment to sit down and open a book (Thanks for choosing this one by the way!), you must have been able to take a break, after an exhausting day of tending your kids, from the stresses of work, or from the endless list of other responsibilities. You are riding the waves of exhaustion right along with me.

Most likely, if I have time to open a book or magazine, it's because I have locked myself in the bathroom for a few moments of peace and quiet while in a bath. The water is usually lukewarm, and half of the bubbles have already dissipated by the time I am finally able to get in and relax. This is because after I announce that I am heading to the bathtub and my family sees a book in my hand, each individual suddenly *needs* something urgently.

Because of my present state in life as a wife, mom, full-time employee, and writer, I usually nod off a few minutes into even the best book. As you can probably imagine, my nap only lasts a few moments because the water becomes too cold, I don't want to risk pruning up or hypothermia, or someone comes screaming through the door requiring Mom, and only Mom, to open another package of fruit snacks.

So yeah, I'm tired. It's more of an overall, general state of being these days. I'm sure that you can understand.

It's only 1:45 p.m. on a Friday. I'm contemplating a second cup of coffee already. I have to pick up my kids from school in an hour. If I'm not early, I won't get a parking spot that they can actually see me from. Then they will be standing there looking at a long line of minivans and large SUVs with worry in their eyes, thinking that Mom has forgotten to pick them up.

Even when I do get to school on time, I sit in my car and wave frantically to my kids, hoping that they will see me from where they are standing so that I don't have to get out and retrieve them from their classes' lines. What others see of me through my car window is a mom who looks put together, has curled hair, and is wearing a tunic sweater.

But what they don't see is that my hair hasn't been washed today and that I'm wearing sweat pants that don't match my sweater, black socks, and teal sport sandals—an improvement from the slippers I had on before. I changed them because I thought my kids would be mortified if I left the house with them on. Now that I look down and see my ensemble, they will probably be more mortified with my socks and sandals' choice.

So no, I don't want to get out of my car in front of Flawless Fran, Pinterest Polly, and Instagram Ivy. With their perfectly applied lip gloss on and wearing designer sunglasses, they walk across the parking lot to chat politely with the teacher before picking up their children and walking them back to their rust-free vans with no-smudge windows. They smile down at their children and admire their latest pieces of artwork.

Meanwhile, I am yelling at my children, "Hurry up and get in! Oh, my goodness, you guys need haircuts, like *now!* You look homeless." Then off we go to the walk-in salon across the street for discount haircuts.

Today, I'm craving another cup of coffee because my delicious pumpkin-cream cold brew coffee from this morning held me over until about 11:30 a.m. and just before my toddler's tantrum over what I was serving for lunch. She asked for macaroni and cheese—until it was served to her. Then, all of the sudden, she *hated* mac and cheese.

Usually, that second cup of caffeine is a late-afternoon decision. On some nights when I'm seven hours into my ten-hour shift, I pull out that small container of pink, caffeinated powder and watch it fall into the water. I think about how sweet it will taste and how its wonderful powers will carry me through to the end of my shift. It's like unicorns, mermaids, and dragons. I see it, and it's so beautiful. I just can't stop thinking about the way that it will give me superpowers to accomplish everything on my to-do list with impressive speed and clarity. All of the other moms will wonder what my secret is.

As I walk through Target, all I will think about until I have one in my hand and sip its frothy wonderfulness is that delicious caramel-colored latte. Its magic powers will fill my veins and give me life.

I am one of those people who drinks 120 milligrams of caffeine before 8 p.m. and then sleeps through the night. Okay, let's be real. I haven't had a full night's sleep in over three years. But you get the point.

Decaf—what's the point? Decaf is for weaklings who only like the taste of coffee. Make it a triple shot. I can handle my caffeine like a professional. Are there professional caffeine drinkers? It is one area of life that I would totally rock at. At least, it feels good to be great at something that doesn't take hard work. I believe that is pretty close to the way that the dictionary would define the word *addiction*.

Black tea is for my sensitive, emotional mornings. Lattes, when I want to relax, but not nap. Cold brew is for a real kick in the pants. Massive amounts of coffee, or Spark, are for those get-up-and-get-stuff-done kinds of days. You name it, and I want it. Would I try matcha tea? Yeah, I would, even though I've heard it tastes like feet. If it's going to get me through the day, I'm sitting high in the no-judgment zone.

Mugs fill two entire shelves of my kitchen cupboard. I have the plain, boring ones that come in a set of eight. Some of my mugs are beautifully painted with delicate flowers and lettering, which I save for when I'm in the mood for a cup of hot English Breakfast tea. I have some that have been decorated with sharpie by my kindergartener. My most special mugs come from my most favorite places around the country, and they say things like, "Virginia," "Estes Park," and "Holland." When I sip a latte in one of those mugs, I imagine I am in that place with a sibling or friend. I have a mug for any mood and caffeine craving.

This brings me to a burning question, which I have been too afraid to ask. But here it goes. Is there such a thing as too much caffeine? So far, I have handled life and gotten through each day by riding a fine line between just-enough and too-much-now-my-heart-is-palpating caffeine. It controls whether I lose my cool or handle all of those little people and the decisions that they need me to make. We all have to make it through the day somehow. For me, it's with a big cup of coffee and a whole lot of Jesus.

I know you're with me. You feel me. You're tipping your cup and giving me that wink because you know that I dry shampooed my hair again and put on the same sweatpants as yesterday. You're smiling because you woke up this morning and did it too.

You're the person that I call and cry to when I feel like I've failed again. You're the one I meet for coffee and a walk at the farmers' market. We don't buy anything, but we spend our time talking about the things that we would buy if we knew what a *chard* was or the way to prepare a purple cauliflower. You're the one I call when I have a hankering for Mexican food.

You are my sisters, my friends, my mother, and my gram. You are the women that I work with, who remind me why we do what we do. You are the stranger on social media that I pull strength and courage from. You're a mom and a wife, or you just have a caffeine addiction too.

Whoever you are as you sit on the other side of this book, I'm glad you are here with me. We both came to this space to fill our cups, figuratively speaking and in my case, literally. So I hope you will grab a cup of your favorite brew and stay with me through these pages as we navigate this wild, wonderful life.

I bet when you opened a book today, you didn't know that you'd be making a new friend. Well, guess what, friend, you just did.

Hey, New Friend

So you got a new book and gained a new friend. Maybe you didn't ask for either one. But here I am pushing my way into your life. The only way to stop it is not to read another word. But aren't you even a little curious to find out what your interesting new friend has to say to you?

I'm going to do my best to keep you here for two reasons. First, I like you already. Second, at thirty-five years old, I have come to realize how important meaningful connections and friendships are. They may be other moms, wives, coworkers, grandmas, or the lady next door. They are women whom you can count on, and they can count on you.

Why do we need them? Why do you need me and I need you? When I go to my husband and cry about the way that I was defeated by an epic toddler tantrum in the middle of the grocery store *after* realizing that my shirt was on inside out and unleashing my wrath on a barista who gave me sugar-free syrup instead of regular, my husband looks at me and says, "Why do you let her do that? She never throws a tantrum for me." We all know that my rage monster has now been released by his pity.

My well-meaning husband now fears for his life because that was *not* what I *needed*. I need many things from my husband, and he is very good at providing those things. But sometimes there have been moments when I have been defeated by the little humans that he can somehow manage to bring to obedience. He doesn't always understand what I need, but my friends do.

My friends understand that one little three-year-old can make me lose my mind in less than thirty seconds. When that happens, I need to call one of them, vent about how rotten my toddler was, and gush about how much I love her, all in the same breath.

Then with tears still in my eyes, I listen to her say, "Yeah, that happened to me last week, and guess what? I forgot to put on underwear before leaving the house."

Then we laugh and compete with each other about which one of us is the bigger slob and space cadet. We make plans to grab a coffee and take the kids to the park later in the week, and *bam,* life seems better again and my grocery store nightmare is nothing because only my friend would forget to put on panties before leaving her house.

My friends are awesome. Just as my husband, I need them too.

It wasn't until I was well into adulthood that I actually learned how to be a friend. I know that sounds weird. You may be wondering if I spent my childhood alone, humming to myself, and locked in my bedroom. No, but childhood friendships are all the same.

They are about riding bikes around the neighborhood, having lemonade stands in the driveway, and fighting over whose Barbie gets to be the mom and live with the one-and-only Ken. That means someone else's Barbie has to live with her cats and go to work. By the way, there was nothing wrong with that, especially since Barbie always had a supercool job like an astronaut or a veterinarian. But before we grew up and realized that being an independent career woman was cool, everyone wanted to marry Ken.

Here's the thing. I moved a lot as a kid. Even moving once as a preteen, when life is already tough and awkward, adjusting to a new school and making friends can seem like a nightmare that a person can't wake up from. I made friends easily and quickly when I started a new school, and I had a lot of them. It was the way that I survived. I would be accommodating, do what they wanted me to do, and survive the school year.

My high school friendships were solid. Every weekend, we had sleepovers where we ate pepperoni and black olive pizza, applied sparkly blue nail polish, and gossiped about boys. Shopping trips included spending hard-earned tips on ear piercings and nose rings. We spent nights crying together over the crush that didn't like me back, and we prank-called the boys from our class. I thought those friendships would last a lifetime.

But I learned after high school that I was just a *yes* friend. I would say, "Yes," to anyone and everything, just to have friends that liked and wanted me around. It was never anything dangerous like drugs, sex, alcohol or that would get me in serious trouble or break the law. Although, these choices did earn me the demeaning title of Goody Two-shoes, up until graduation.

There were a few times when I did say, "No." A least I knew how to give the I-didn't-hear-you look, turn, and walk away. Usually, I did this because I knew the butt-whooping that I would receive if I broke the rules would definitely not be worth it. I wasn't that brainless.

I was friends with some really great people, and even though our lives have gone in different directions, they are still really great people. The girls that I counted on to be by my side in high school were everything a hormonal teen could ask for in a friend. But I wasn't that to them. It may have seemed that I was a good friend because I always said, "Yes," to this plan or that idea, but I was not being 100 percent authentic. I was only there to make everyone else happy, even if it meant that I wasn't.

I told myself the lie that I wasn't enough and that I didn't measure up unless my friends were happy and wanted to keep being my friend. I believed it for a long time. I believed it until I wasn't happy with whom I was. I began to loathe myself, and that is a very dark path to be on. It led to hate, self-harm, and resentment. It took getting my little teenage heart broken to crawl out of that hole and learn who I wanted to be: respected, loved, valued, and 100 percent authentic.

So how do you break that thought process and develop meaningful, lasting friendships? That secret is a chapter entirely to itself. But here's the short answer: Be authentic. Would those old friendships have lasted if I had just been real? Yes, I think that they would have. The friendships that I have now at thirty-five are strong and meaningful because I'm me, yep, just me. Take or leave me. This is what you get.

Many people don't care for me, and that's okay. I say that it's quality over quantity. I do not need to be liked. I need to be me—the one and only me that God created to be a specific person. I have new and old friends. The one thing that they all know about me is that I am exactly who I am when we become friends.

Certainly, I am not trying to make people happy by what I am saying. No, but I am trying to do what God wants. If I were still trying to make people happy, I would not be Christ's servant. (Galatians 1:10 EASY)

I am 100 percent intensely caffeinated and authentically working to be the person that God made me to be.

The Not So Secret, Secret

If you are waiting for some profound secret that will change the course of your life, I am sorry to disappoint you. I don't have *that* secret. But I will drop some knowledge on you, and it will change the course of every relationship that you have. Every single relationship you have in your life—spouse, kids, friends, coworkers, parents, and in-laws—can be great, enriching, and fulfilling. It all depends on who you are.

Are you being authentically you? Don't hate me for loving the *authentic*. What does it mean? Look inside yourself. Who are you? Are you happy with whom you are? If not, did you know that you are the only one who can make a change? God will bring out your full potential when you are ready to embrace it. Then you will become everything that you were designed to be—the real unapologetic you. It has taken me years to learn this.

Let me ask you another question. Who sets the tone in your house? If your family is anything like mine, I'm guessing that it's Mom that sets the tone. In my house, if Mom ain't happy, everybody else runs and hides. My attitude can very quickly affect all the other attitudes in the house.

Let me tell you that my attitude can nose-dive quickly. It can be something as simple as my husband not hearing the question that I ask him or walking into my kids' room, right after they told me they had it cleaned up, and finding four random socks, thirteen Nerf bullets, a stack of baseball cards, and one damp bath towel still lying on the floor.

Once my attitude has changed from positive to take cover because Mom's gonna blow, there are only two things that can change it. One is a time-out for Mom. Give her a freshly brewed cup of coffee and not the one that has been warmed up three times because I've been interrupted all morning and haven't finished it. Dump that one out. I don't deserve reheated, stale coffee. Oftentimes, when they finally find me hiding in my closet in mommy time-out, my attitude hasn't really changed. I only got a few minutes of solitude. And secondly, prayer. A lot of sincere prayer.

So try this. Drop to your knees and ask God to change your heart to a tender one and to give you a calm resolve. Do not ask for patience unless you want to receive it by being tested. I have done this before. After asking, I wondered if God was even listening. I was losing the battle as my children fought and tore the house apart. Then the epiphany came to me. *Ah, I see what you did there. Well played*, God, I thought.

As you slowly rise up from your knees, count to ten. Then turn around and apologize to those little cherubs. If this is the first time you have ever done this, grab your camera. You will want to record the look on their faces. Now promise them that you will work on not raising your voice. Next time, remember that promise and keep your cool in the midst of life trying to knock you down.

It is in our natures to become stressed over just about anything and everything. Stress causes tension. Tension causes hostility. Do you see the cycle? Break it. Life will go on if you sit down to watch a movie with the family and there are still dishes in the sink. Life will still go on if you decide to take the kids to the park instead of switching the laundry, which causes you to have to start the washer again when you get home with the same load of damp laundry sitting in it.

Recently my husband told me, during one of my more hostile moments, "Why do you get mad so easily? You get worked up about the littlest things." Granted I had gone from zero to ninety-five on the hostility meter in about thirty seconds. Why had I done it? I don't remember. But it made him crabby, it made the kids crabby, and it made me crabby that they were now crabby. I didn't see it as he did. So after my quick prayer and counting to ten, I asked him to videotape me the next time I reacted that way. If I don't see the thing that I do that affects everyone around me, I can't change it.

As the tone setter of the house, if you want peace, be peaceful. If you want joy, be joyful. If your kids see your positive attitude, they will mirror that positivity. This might not be true of teenagers. I'm not there yet, so I don't know about them. I will be soon, so send me all your tips. I hope you get the idea.

I once asked my kids, "Am I a good mom?" First, the youngest didn't understand the question. She asked for a waffle, threw a fit, and refused to eat it. The oldest said, "Yes?" answering my question with a question. Leave it to the middle child to finally answer my question honestly with a, "Yeah, kinda. You could play games with me more and toys and have fun with us. Be happy more and laugh."

Bam! Wow, right when I thought I was doing those things already. But what he sees is a stressed out mom who doesn't laugh enough, a busy mom who doesn't have enough time to play, and an all-too-often angry mom who doesn't stop to have fun and enjoy her children in the little moments that matter.

If you want to make a positive change, ask the people you live with if you are a good mom, spouse, or person. They are the ones who see you at your worst and deserve you at your best. Listening to their truth about you will be all it will take to stir the change inside yourself.

Change is hard. Believe me; it is easier to be on edge, stressed, and overwhelmed, but it is worth all the trouble and hard work to become the person that God made you to be.

The Man

$\mathcal{T}$ he man, the myth, and the legend—or at least he is to me. He's my husband, Josh. Maybe you thought I was going to say Jason Momoa, Chris Pratt, or one of the Hemsworth brothers. With two young boys and a nerdy husband, I know every superhero. I have a completely innocent mom-crush on Aquaman, Star-Lord, and Thor. But none of them returned my calls, texts, or multiple emails for an interview for this chapter, so this one is all about our own superhero.

I'm going to spend the next few pages bragging about this guy that I've known for eighteen years now—or is it nineteen years? He is the man that I met under very unlikely circumstances. We quickly knew that we would spend a lifetime together.

It was the summer before my senior year of high school. I was seventeen. I planned to spend the summer having sleepovers with my friends, working as a waitress, and spending my tips at the mall. I had a boyfriend, but it was one of those see-you-at-school types of relationships. We didn't really see each other outside of school.

The day I met the man of my dreams, I was doing what every high school girl in the early 2000s did during summer break: shopping. We were at the mall. I was shopping for a new summer swimsuit. One friend was debating on getting her ears pierced again. Another friend wanted a free makeover from the Lancome counter of Younkers.

So two of us sipped our freshly squeezed lemonade and ate our pretzel bites while we waited on the bench outside of Younkers to see our friend's new makeover, when a boy came up to us and started talking. I disinterestedly looked at him and sipped my drink.

He smiled and said, "My friends and I noticed you girls shopping and thought you looked like nice girls, and we wanted to know if you'd want to get ice cream with us?"

Other women my age will understand how this kind of meeting could happen. I thank the stars that we didn't have to date during the social-media age. Nope, we met on mall benches and talked to strangers face-to-face. I didn't even own a cell phone in high school. Gah! I know.

I about choked on my lemonade and said, "Ugh, no! We don't even know you."

My friend was embarrassed, she politely said to him, "Thank you for the offer. That was really sweet of you."

When he shrugged his shoulders and walked away, she turned to me and said, "You were mean. He was so nice and kinda cute. And I kinda want to go get ice cream with them."

"Are you for real? We don't even know them. What if they are creeps?"

"Cool your jets. They won't be. I want to go," she pleaded.

I relented. "Ugh, whatever . But I'm driving, so when I say it's time to go, then we go."

She clapped and giggled, and we went to have ice cream with boys we didn't know. I knew that if my parents found out, I would get the butt-whooping of a lifetime.

As soon as we sat down with those boys for ice cream, I silently thanked my friend for pressuring me to go because I had just lain eyes on the cutest boy that I had ever seen. I hadn't seen him but only his friend while shopping at the mall. It wasn't until I was sitting across from him that I looked into his light blue eyes and got lost like a dreamy-eyed girl who has just met her charming prince.

While he was talking, it was as if everyone else around us had disappeared and we were the only two people in the restaurant. We talked for hours. He was a year older than I was. He would be heading to college soon. He had a good job. He liked the same things that I liked. He was very attractive. I blushed and stared all night long. Then when I finally realized that I had missed curfew by several hours, I rushed home in a happy daze and received my punishment for breaking curfew with a smile on my face, which only made the punishment worse.

He bravely called to check up on me. He was brave because this was back before we all had cell phones, and he had to call our landline. He profusely apologized for talking so much and making me late for curfew. He was sweet and kind, and he truly cared about how I was doing. He was clearly not the type of guy (like others I had been with) who went out with a girl hoping to get something out of it.

We talked every day for a couple weeks, During that time, I ended my relationship with my high school boyfriend, whom I never saw because it was now summer. Before long, we began our summer relationship. We saw each other and talked on the phone every day. I quickly knew that I was in love and that I had never felt that way before. He said it first, but I said it back to him on the following day. I left him with increasing anxiety for twenty-four hours.

As summer was nearing an end and he would be leaving for college soon, I knew that we could make long distance work. There was no doubt that he was the person that I was meant to be with, so we could survive the time apart during our college years. But his fears got the best of him, and he broke it off right before leaving for school. Of course, I was devastated, but a little glimmer of hope still burned inside of me. So I waited for him … patiently.

We only spoke once during his first six months of school, and it was excruciating. He wanted advice about a girl that he liked, and her name was Laura too. Ugh, what gall he had. But I still waited. I knew our story wasn't done yet.

Over Christmas break, I went shopping at the mall with my friend to spend my Christmas money. That's when I saw him. I hadn't seen him in six months, and just like that, there he was. He was more handsome than I remembered him being. It might have been because he was a college boy now.

I didn't know what to say or do. Would he still care as I did? Our eyes locked, and he came up to me. We chatted and agreed to get together before his break was over.

Later that same day, he called and admitted that he had made the worst mistake of his life when he had let me go. He had realized it immediately after he had broken it off. He assumed that he had ruined having any chance of a future with me, until he saw me that day in the mall. Just like that, we were together again and stronger than before. We talked about our future and ways that we would help our relationship survive the long distance during our college years.

Years later after we were already engaged, he told me something that I will never forget because it was the sweetest most-romantic thing I've ever heard. It was romantic like the movie *The Notebook*. That's how good it was. He swept me off my feet again when he told me. He said that the night we had met, he had been driving home with his friends after having ice cream, and had had said to them, "Guys, this is going to sound off the wall, and I don't know how I know this, but … someday I'm going to marry that girl," and that he did.

The Marriage

$\mathcal{I}$t is fifteen years later, and it has not been all roses. We have overcome some monumental marital hurdles. We have experienced much growth and maturing through our years together, and it has been hard. But it is good—sooooo good.

Let me tell you what I tell all newlyweds. When I heard this piece of advice, I thought, *Oh, that won't be us.* To say the least, I was naive and blindsided. Sister, you can believe that it won't be you, but you should prepare for it anyway. So here it is: Beware of year six. When I was a newlywed, I was warned about the make-it-or-break-it year too, and man, everyone was right. It was definitely the point in our marriage when we came to a big fork in the road. We had to make a very difficult decision: Fight for it or walk away.

When you are pregnant, people give you all sorts of unsolicited advice. The number one thing that I heard all the time when I was pregnant was, "Being a parent is the hardest job you will ever do." That's wrong! Being a spouse is the hardest job you will ever have. When you bring a child into the world or into a family, that child grows up knowing the people who will love, protect, and care for them forever. When you enter into a marriage, you don't have the same assurances. You hope those things will always be true. They are promised, but they are never guaranteed.

So, you wake up every morning and look at the person lying next to you, and decide again to love them, and that you are also worth their love. Most days, it is not a question of whether that special person loves you or not, and it takes very little to convince you to love them back. Your spouse chooses to love you each day, but he or she does not have to. Their love is not required. It is a choice they make each day they are with you.

The hardest job is loving, and asking for love in return, learning how to fight well (Yes, it really happens), compromising on all sorts of things you never thought you would, and sharing all the responsibilities. This can take many, many years to figure out like it did for us. I want you to know this in case no one has said it to you before.

This now brings me to the beginning of my marriage. We were a couple of young kids who had just moved in together. We returned home from our tiny honeymoon to our tiny two-bedroom apartment. Yep, we had to figure out how to live with each other *after* our wedding. We learned along the way, and we are still learning every day.

For the first year or two, it was easy and wonderful. His little quirks weren't annoying at all. He would throw his dirty socks in the middle of the living room floor, leave every cupboard door open after getting into it, and use my hair dryer and not put it away, which he still does today. Oh, how cute I used to think those things were. Ha! That lasted a minute.

By year three and four of our marriage, all we did was fight about the little quirks that both of us had. They were no longer cute. Those things were now driving us up the wall. I thought, *Why doesn't he ever pick up his socks from the floor?* He wondered why I always left the lights on in the basement or kitchen at night. Again and again, we fought about the same things. It was exhausting. It drained us of energy, love, and patience.

We still had good times, made memories, laughed, and enjoyed being with each other. But the bad days were always the same. We had the same silly fights about the same insignificant things, which we had already fought over a hundred times.

Maybe you are in a new relationship or marriage, and you are thinking, *Those aren't silly fights. That would drive me insane too!* I agree. Obviously, I totally get it because I wasted so much time fighting about those things.

But then the fighting stopped. That's when the real problems began. When you stop fighting about the things you have always fought about, are the problems resolved, or have you just given up? This is what year six is.

The same things still bothered me, but it was too exhausting to fight about it anymore. The same things were still annoying, but I couldn't change him, and he couldn't change me. Those little annoyances had grown into so much more than the little things that they were really about. They now festered between us and caused resentment. We were no longer fighting about any of it. We were hardly talking at all.

We both spent more time with friends than we did together.

When we did talk, it was an occasional explosive fight in front of those friends. Basically, we had gotten to a point where we were no longer a loving married couple. We were roommates who barely tolerated each other and silently passed each other in the hall.

The worst part was that we had one small child stuck in the middle of our misery. We both knew that we wanted another baby. But at that point, we wondered how that would ever be possible in a failing marriage.

Then the breaking point came. During one of those explosive fights that wasn't even about the things that we were yelling about. He asked me the question that I think I had been dreading. "Do you even love me anymore?"

There was a long pause, and then I replied, "Yes, I still love you. But I don't *like* who you are anymore. I don't like who I am. And I definitely don't like what we have become."

It was quiet in the room. We had finally stopped yelling.

Then he said, "I agree. I feel the same. So what do we do now?"

There it was; the fork in the road. In that moment—or even the months or year building up to that moment—we felt like it might be easier and a relief to call it quits and just part ways. But neither of us went into our marriage commitment ever believing that we would quit. So we chose the only other option we had on the table: Fight as if everything that truly matters depends on it.

Let me explain the basics of how we got to that point, without sending you running in the opposite direction from the idea of marriage. We were poor communicators with each other. We both made some poor choices. We didn't show each other respect, which led us to feeling hurt and angry. My ideas and goals for the future were different from his, and his differed from mine. Our future dreams were not being built together in unity. We felt alone.

To all the married people who are reading this, I guarantee you will relate to at least some of this. Marriage is great. It can be really great. But it is also the hardest job that I have ever done. It is so hard that you will sometimes think about putting in your two-week notice and walking away. For every reason that I have had to walk away, I have had ten or even one hundred reasons to stay and put effort into it. I don't want to only make it work, but I want to make it better.

We chose to fight for the marriage that we wanted and not the one that we had. It was uncomfortable and hard. We occasionally reverted to our old ways. Sometimes we still wanted to give up, but we persisted.

It took us at least into year seven to climb out of our dark hole and begin to see the light of this new marriage that we were building. Over time, we have learned more about ourselves, each other, and what we want our marriage and family to be. It's definitely not perfect. But we frequently look back to that time and remind each other that we never want to get to that point again. We definitely don't want to go back to the way things were before that time either.

We have learned how to make compromises. The socks (and now hats) don't bother me anymore. The annoying things that I do, like leaving lights on at night, either don't bother him, or he chooses to let it go. We know that there are certain things that we can't change about the other person and that we have to learn to let them go. We cannot let those little things destroy the big thing: us.

We have learned the way to fight effectively. Wow! That one sounds like an oxymoron, but it actually works most of the time. We still have plenty of fights that include me blocking the bedroom door, trapping my silent, angry husband, and talking *at* him until he is so aggravated that he finally spews his frustrations. Then we can actually yell it out and maybe come to a one-sided, resentful resolution.

This happens when I'm trying to avoid the alternative or in other words, the way he chooses to fight. He stews in silence for two days while my blood pressure continues to rise. He eventually gets over our fight and goes back to life as normal without talking about it at all. So I have to decide which one is better.

Neither fighting style works for us. Through a lot of hurt, we learned the way to do it better. It still takes a lot of practice. Most importantly, we must be intentional about the way that we handle conflict when it comes up.

When things "hit the fan", I especially have to step back and think, *Am I mad at him or the situation?* Usually, it's the situation, and there are things that have led up to it. Before I blow up, I need to give him a moment to explain. By the time that he's explained, not only have I calmed down some but I also understand his side of the situation a little better. Then instead of blowing my top, we can talk about the reason that we are frustrated and what we need to do about it.

It's not a perfect system. There are still plenty of times when I revert to yelling, storming off, or slamming doors. Yes, I know. Even at thirty-five, I can still slam a door that screams spit and fire. My stubbornness runs in the family, unfortunately.

NOTES FROM GRAM ON MARRIAGE

I like to think of marriage as a progression. It's like attending school from kindergarten through college.

The first years are exciting. You experience twenty-four-hour love, whether you are miles apart or together in the same house. You don't just have your individual lifestyle anymore because everything is a *we* event.

The next phase is parenthood. Whether it is the first year or the tenth, if you are lucky enough to be a part of this miracle, your life changes because you're not only responsible for overseeing your kids' care, but you must teach safety, sharing, good health habits, proper diet, and more. You must ask them if they brushed their teeth and used the potty. During this period, marriage takes a back seat, but getting in the back seat once in a while earns you a gold star. Don't ever stop having fun moments alone like in the falling-in-love days.

Before you even stop to count, the years have passed. You managed to cut the apron strings. Don't be tempted to leave them within pulling distance. Children need to learn by experience. Sometimes, they don't make wise decisions, but erase, "I told you so," from your vocabulary. They probably already recall that advice anyway.

It is a cycle if you are lucky. Empty nesters can return to the magic of a perfect union. You have both matured, are more tolerant, and can read each other's thoughts. The fascination you felt for each other in your dating years has turned into a perfect union.

The Second Hardest Job

*W*hy are some children such fearless, reckless daredevils? It seems that they are either fearless or scared of everything—every shadow, sound, and creepy crawling thing.

But this one is surprisingly not about one of those little humans being reckless. It's about a kid who falls and lands wrong *three times*. I'm going to wrap him in bubble wrap. I can't handle any more broken bones. Who is that breakable? He had three broken arms before middle school. Who does that? Okay, he gets it from me.

If we were keeping score, my tiny, middle child and I are in a tie. We say a quick prayer after every fall and wait for him to bounce back up, declaring, "I'm okay!"

On this particular day, it was broken arm number three. As I turned the corner onto our street, I immediately saw the look on my husband's face. His hands came up to his head, as he stood at the car door where my youngest son was strapped in. He looked overwhelmed.

My first thought was that my husband and my son were fighting, but as I get closer, I saw the fear on my husband's face. I rolled down my window as I get closer and shouted, "What's the matter?"

He replied, "Jackson broke his arm again."

"What? Again? Are you sure?"

"Oh yes, it's definitely broken."

Without hesitating, I yelled for him to get back in his car, where the boys were already strapped in, and go to the hospital. I didn't take the time to get out of my own vehicle. I had my toddler with me. We left. We would just have to have two cars at the ER.

When we got to the hospital, I saw him cradled in my husband's arms. He was crying with his big blue eyes squeezed tight and his hand clutching his injured arm. I didn't actually see the arm until we got into a room.

As soon as my husband let go of him, I thought, *Yep. Broken. Definitely broken.* His poor little arm was bent where it wasn't supposed to bend. Tears filled my eyes, and I had to look away from his arm. I looked into his eyes instead. They were wet and red.

I told him over and over to look at me while the nurses worked around him, giving him pain meds and taking vitals. They were amazing nurses. They were so gentle and worked quickly to take his pain away and make him comfortable.

They were there for me just as much as they were for him, but they didn't even know it. They didn't know that their gentle touches, soothing voices, and quick actions were calming me. I focused on my little man, talked to him, and rubbed his hair while they were busy doing tests and talking to doctors.

I'm not the only one who cried and wished to take his pain away. Dad held his hand while he was asleep and his bones were reset. With tears running down his cheeks, his big brother was in the hall silently praying for his little brother and best friend. His sweet little sister wiped tears away with a Kleenex and planted kisses on her injured brother.

This is the scary part of having children. You do everything you can every day to keep them safe. Then they just fall.

We've been down this road so many times now that I now

know what my parents went through with me. Each time seems worse, or at least, it's not any easier than the previous time.

When he cried each day because he couldn't stop thinking about his bent arm and his fear that when the cast came off, it would still be bent, I would do anything to take it all away from him. He asked me to sit and pray with him because he was scared, and he wanted comfort. I sat with him and prayed. Then I prayed some more in the quietness of my room because parenting was hard, and I too needed comfort. I'd endure it all for him if it meant he wouldn't have nightmares about the break anymore.

That is the reason that it is the second hardest job. How many hours of sleep are lost worrying about our kids' safety? We have the doctor on speed dial so that every time there is a fever or cough, we can quickly call. We worry about grades, friends, that they are getting too much screen time, and that they aren't getting enough vegetables in their diets. Should we homeschool them, send them to private school, or have them go to public school?

No one has the perfect answers to all parenting questions. The only *right* way to parent is by loving, providing for, protecting, and caring for them and nurturing their minds and souls. Give those things to them, and then give yourself grace because you are doing a great job. Your kids will be fine. Yes, there will still be hurdles, attitudes, rule breaking, and too many emotions. But that comes with every child right out of the womb.

Parenting is tough, and rewarding. But believe me, it ages you faster than you can imagine. I'm thirty-five, and I started covering my gray hair ten years ago. The first ones grew in right after my first baby was born. Was this a coincidence? It's doubtful.

But as they say, "This too shall pass." This is true of all life's tough circumstances, including parenting. It may pass like a kidney stone, but it will pass.

The Story of the Broken Arm

By Jackson While in the Fourth Grade

Warning: This story gets wild!

Chapter 1

Hello, I'm Jack, and I'm going to tell you a story. It all started out as only me getting into the car. I was going to get a new baseball glove with Dad. I hadn't been able to play much because of all of those other broken arms. But I wasn't getting a glove that day. My dad was surprising me, and we were going to a movie instead. We were finally going to see the new Marvel movie. I was getting into the car when …

Chapter 2

Long story short, I slipped out of the car and *broke my arm*. It really hurt. I said, "Ahhhhhhh!" I was put to sleep. I had a Pokemon dream. I woke up with a …

Chapter 3

Cast and sling. It took about eight weeks for it to heal. There was no baseball, swimming, and trampoline jumping all summer. After that, my arm felt weird. I learned not to brace myself with straight arms, after breaking it three times.

The Mom Uniform

When I was *much* younger, I remember thinking that I was going to be one of those hip, trendy moms. I was going to wear the trendy jeans that everyone, including the hottest celebrities, was wearing. I had planned to wear lots of stylish jewelry, and for years, I bought a lot of it, only to leave it sitting in a drawer. I dreamed of my future daughter begging to borrow my clothes and playing for hours in my closet because she envied my stylish taste.

Ha! I am not that mom. Now that I am a real adult with a busy job and a million hours a week of parenting, I dream of putting on my favorite pair of sweatpants and an oversized sweatshirt on the weekends. I'm usually braless, if I have no plans to leave the house.

Recently, my best friend told me that I'd probably be the only person she had ever known to be buried in sweatpants when I died. That's why she is my best friend. She knows me, and she can joke with me about my wardrobe … and my death.

Last Saturday night, my husband and I were invited to a friend's big milestone birthday. That meant date night, which I'm sad to say, only happens about once a year. We booked the babysitter two months in advance, and she was spending the night so that we would be able to to stay out as late as we wanted.

Then I was told it was a formal night, with elegant dresses, fancy jewelry, and high heels. All I had in my closet under that category was five bridesmaids' dresses dating back eleven years. I didn't want to buy something that I would wear once and then have it sit in my closet forever, so I had to get creative and be very resourceful. It wasn't my typical faded sweatpants and inspirational T-shirt, but I pulled it off.

We cleaned up nice. I got a bunch of compliments on my dress, and we had a wonderful night out with friends. The birthday girl even commented, "Wow, you're not wearing sweatpants."

To which I sarcastically replied, "Don't worry, I have them on under my dress."

I'd like to share a quick how to achieve a formal look for

those of you who are reading this, and like me, don't know how to be fancy.

THE DRESS

What's most important is having a classy mom, grandma, aunt, or friend who has much better style and taste and obviously values beautiful clothes more than you and your ten-year-old sweatpants do. Raid her closet. Stay out of yours.

So yes, my beautiful evening gown was my mom's gown. This amazing woman has about twenty of them just hanging in her closet and begging to be worn again. I felt like Anne Hathaway walking into her palace closet in *The Princess Diaries*. I walked in there and tried on dress after dress in front of full-length mirrors. I twirled, spun, and tossed them in a yes or no pile.

Don't forget deodorant. Apply it liberally. Remember, it's not your dress.

SHOES

After you've tried on every pair of ultra-high heels from your mom's closet and realized that your feet no longer bend that way, grab the last pair from your closet that you wore to a wedding. It doesn't matter anyway because no one will see them under the dress.

JEWELRY

Pull out what you wore to the last two weddings. With a hairstyle that is down or swept to the side, it's okay to only wear one earring. This in the likely event of your ear becoming red and sore because you never wear earrings, or you've lost one since the last wedding.

HANDBAG

If you have a date, don't be concerned about it because you don't need one. He should have at least six pockets on him.

THE HAIR

Touch up your curls from yesterday. Pin back the unruly ones.

MAKEUP

Dig out the black eyeliner that you are too scared to wear. Carefully apply your used fake eyelashes if you ran out of mascara. Wear lipstick only if you find a tube less than two years old or one that hasn't been "gooped" up by a three-year-old playing princess.

Your total look comes to zero dollars. This is my favorite kind of deal, even though, you may end up with pink eye and a red earlobe from earrings you never wear. People might also talk about how nice it was to see you in something other than sweatpants. But rocking your mom's evening gown and getting asked by your three-year-old if you are a real princess is priceless.

Getting a night out on the town with a handsome man who is dressed to the nines, you wearing a beautiful gown, and having a babysitter stay all night are just what every busy parent needs every now and again. The idea of dinner at a fancy restaurant that doesn't include chicken nuggets and chocolate milk on the bill sounds like a dream. You want to soak up every child-free moment of a quiet dinner.

That is true until about 10:30 p.m. Then your body reminds you that you don't know how to party and stay up past 9:00 p.m. anymore, and it's time to be a responsible adult and go home to bed.

I experienced this, went home, and soaked my sore high-heeled feet in hot water. I spent the rest of the weekend in sweatpants.

Don't forget about leggings. Yes, they totally qualify as pants if

1. They are not see-through.
2. Your shirt is long enough to cover the goods.
3. They aren't printed with children's cartoon characters. This is also not okay for pajama pants, unless of course you are three years old.

It's three babies later, and I have an obvious mom-bod. Leggings and sweatpants are my complete wardrobe. Forget jeans. They are no longer my friends. They are cute pants of betrayal.

Don't Burn the Banana Bread

*W*hen I'm asked, "How was your day?" my typical response is, "Busy." I'm usually thinking about the next thing that I need to do or the next place we need to be. This is quickly followed by my trying to reassure myself that, yes, I'm busy, but I shouldn't worry because next week won't be as hectic. That is a lie because seriously, when has that ever been true?

Today, I had good intentions of doing the washing, folding, and putting away laundry. It's needed to be done for three days now.

But then I remember the fridge is empty, so I need to buy groceries. Then there's the birthday present that needs to be wrapped before tomorrow. Then I get invited out to lunch. If I prioritize well, the youngest can still get a nap in before we leave the house again.

This reminds me that her car seat was full of crumbs and raisins when I got her out of it earlier. I'll have to take it out and vacuum the seats. It hasn't been vacuumed all winter, so I'll vacuum the floors too. Maybe I should just run the whole thing through the carwash.

I better get the chicken out and marinated before we leave for lunch so that it'll be ready when we come home. Lunch will be relaxing, and then maybe, we will do a little shopping.

Did I seriously think I could sit down and enjoy my lunch out with a toddler? Instead of eating her grilled cheese sandwich, she holds it as she walks around and around the table. Then she continues to hold it and nibbles birdie bites from it an hour later in her stroller while I shop.

It's definitely time to go home. I need to get at least one load of laundry done today, except I didn't keep track of the time. Now I have to pick up the boys from school.

They desperately need haircuts again. Where's that coupon? If these cuts go quickly, I can catch up on a little laundry before the piano recital tonight.

Oh, I forgot about those bananas in the fridge that I was going to use for banana bread. Of course, I'm out of sugar, oil, and vanilla. I'll have to send my husband to the store now.

That's when I tweak my knee. All of the sudden, I can't move it without terrible pain. So I'll just sit here with an ice pack until recital time. I'll put the bread in the oven when we get back.

Finally at 8:30 p.m., all of the kids are tucked in and the bread is in the oven. Whew! We crawl into bed and turn on the TV. I pray that I won't fall asleep before the oven timer goes off. We lie there silently watching the baby monitor. Our little girl burrows under her blanket as we hear giggles coming from the bunk bed across the hall.

I think about the day and how busy it was. I'm not even the least bit surprised that I didn't get to the laundry. Because let's face it, most days are like this, and it's not going to be any different next week. We may not have clean socks or T-shirts tomorrow, but right now, we do have a happy little girl cuddling her blankie, two brothers making memories while giggling about something secret, and a few quiet moments with my husband before we do it all again the next day.

Of course, we also have banana bread, which I totally burned.

Breakfast has to be cereal and toast again, which brings me to my next topic. Take care of yourself. because let's be real, we will all lose our minds if we don't remember to take a moment out for ourselves.

Don't Neglect Self-Care

*L*ast week, I had a patient who dropped some serious truth into my lap. She was fifty-seven years old with four grown children. Her oldest was thirty-eight. While her son was in the room with her, this patient reminded me that mother's need more than just one Mother's day. We need one day a week or one week a year to be focused on us and taking care of ourselves. I say, "Amen, Mama!"

As her son argued with her logic from the corner of an ER room, I turned to him and said, "Listen. You are in a losing battle here. Your mother is a very wise woman, and she is speaking truth right into my soul."

So here's what happens on my one day a year. I got a wonderfully made breakfast and hot coffee while I was in bed. The kids cleaned up the house, which just meant that I would have to put away the things that they had cleaned into their proper spots later.

I got to take a quiet bath with a new bath bomb. That lasted all of fifteen minutes before my three-year-old busted through the broken, locked bathroom door, stripped, and took over my bath. As she squeezed herself down into the little spot next to my legs, she poked my stomach with her little, wet finger and said too enthusiastically, "Your tummy is so squishy, Mommy!"

I think, *Yes, dear daughter, thank you for that reminder. I hadn't thought of that at all for at least four whole minutes.*

That was my cue to get out. Then my husband sticks his head in and says, "How was your bath?" Seriously? I just roll my eyes as he looks behind me at the little bath stealer, playing with her Barbie.

Mother's day is months behind us now. I have since learned that if I want a completely peaceful bath, it will only happen at about eleven at night when everyone is asleep.

Today is a hot summer Sunday. I have longed for a few quiet minutes to myself this weekend so that I can sit and write. Surprisingly, it takes a little work to get these words flowing.

Usually, it only happens when I shut myself off from the noise in the world. Kids, husband, pets, job, kids' school, and news in the world all consume my thoughts every moment of the day and sometimes even through the night. So when I want to sit quietly and put all of these thoughts on paper, it takes work to get everything else out of my head. Just to find a few minutes in itself is near impossible.

It's in this chapter because it is a form of self-care. I used to be able to run when I wanted to let the stress out, become focused and grounded, and spend a little time in solitude. Well, thanks to an "eighty-five-year old" knee (words straight from my surgeon), I have lost too much cartilage and damaged it from years of running to keep doing it. So I had to find something else to take care of myself, especially my mind because a large part of self-care is mental wellness.

I went through the steps of grief when I quit being able to run. I tried many different things that could potentially replace running as my mental outlet. It has been three and a half years now, and with a lot of encouragement from my gram, writing has become that outlet of self-care.

Just like running, it takes a lot of preparation before it actually happens. I don't have to change clothes, put on running shoes, stretch, and grab my inhaler on the way out the door. But it is still a process to sit down and put the words on paper.

Today I woke up wanting to write. Now it is 2:50 p.m., and I have only been in front of the screen for five songs (about 20 minutes).

I had to get a very whiny, reluctant toddler down for a nap. I had to get another child slathered with sunscreen and ready for the pool so that he could go with his friend. I had to remind my husband to take the movie rental back when he dropped our son off at the pool. Then again, I had to hand it to him when he forgot to grab the movie on the way out of the house. Oh, I had to switch the laundry so that it wouldn't need to go through the wash cycle again.

That all happened in the thirty minutes prior to sitting in front of the laptop. Prepping from early morning for these few moments of self-care meant doing lawn work and cleaning out the baby pool and refilling it, which then brought over the neighbor kids when they heard the water and giggles coming from our deck. I had to plan a meal for dinner, which was a challenge every day when I worked second shift. I had to make sure all the kids actually ate lunch because it was Sunday, and it was no one's job to cook lunch on that day.

Once all of the pieces were in place and all the humans were where they were supposed to be at 2:00 p.m. on that Sunday afternoon, I could finally sit down in front of my machine. But it still wasn't that easy. After all the mommy stress, I had to lift it off me and get into self-care mode. That meant filling my cup literally and figuratively. I filled my Bubba cup to the brim with my current favorite iced coffee. Then I pulled up a Spotify playlist that I thought would resonate deep in my soul and get the words flowing. Now it's 3:00 p.m., and it was just what I needed before heading into Monday and another long work week.

Mama, sister, mother, grandma, and friend, please take care of yourself too. I know you are already taking care of everyone else. Trust me; you can't be at your best unless you are taking care of yourself. No, it's not selfish. It's what the people in your life need you to do.

NOTES FROM GRAM

Self-care is a new word in my vocabulary, but it is quite descriptive. I look back to a couple of generations ago when we had young 'uns. Our main objective was to provide a comfortable home and adequate meals. We took them to church and school. They were happy times. I don't recall worrying about flu outbreaks, and polio had been licked. So there were great times that we didn't realize were happening until we looked back on them because we were too busy to evaluate them.

For our whole family, staying busy was the best self-care we could obtain- and most satisfying. Now back to my generation- my self-care is doing for others. But in the only way I can- correspondence with others, no visiting and no trips to the store due to a pandemic does make it difficult, but I've found my ways of keeping up with it.

So to those who are in the younger generation like you, stop and smell the roses. They are most beautiful and fragrant at this stage of your lives and before driver's licenses, parties, and girlfriends or boyfriends who break hearts.

When I was young, self-care was walking two miles every morning to work or church, which kept me healthy and offered quiet moments for sorting my thoughts or clearing my mind. Nowadays, self-care consists of reading, observing, writing letters and memories like this, knitting, and walking the short distance to the mailbox four times each morning.

Always take care of yourself. You may not realize how important it is until you've reached an age such as mine.

Vacations, Take Them

$\mathcal{I}$t really doesn't matter if you spend the night in your backyard or go on a month-long trek through Europe. Just go. Take a break and get away—and take the kids with you. It doesn't have to be for every trip. I get it, just like every other mom out there does. We need a break from our children for a night or two, every once in a while.

Whether it's a family vacation to the mountains, a romantic getaway with your spouse, or a girls' weekend to a spa and shopping, do it! It doesn't matter if you are working forty hours, eighty hours a week, three jobs, or part time. It doesn't matter if you don't work outside of the home at all. We all need a vacation and deserve a little time away from our normal life—the mundane, routine, and constant cycle. We need to break away from it occasionally, so that we can recharge, reenergize, get back into it all with a new energy and renewed focus, and tackle the everyday things.

I've never been to Disney World, Europe, or even Canada. But I have been to the Rocky and Blue Ridge Mountains several times. I have dipped my toes in the Atlantic Ocean, Gulf of Mexico, and the Great Lakes. I have only been in an airplane a few times. I have driven across the country in a great big van and sat cramped in our family SUV more times than I can count.

The memories I have from those family vacations as a child are not of the touristy things we did or the souvenirs we purchased. The souvenirs collected dust under the mountain of stuff on our dressers and bedroom shelves, if they didn't break before getting them all the way home.

I have memories of six of us in one tent as we camped in the cold damp fog. We peed in the dark woods in the middle of the night. We searched for the bright eyes of nocturnal animals before squatting quickly. I have memories of campfires, stories, and age-old songs. We roasted marshmallows and hot dogs with questionable sticks that we found in the forest.

We sat up in the nosebleed section of the stadium at a baseball game. We shared an overpriced soda and popcorn while squinting at the tiny men on the field.

Taking my own children on family vacations is the same. We treasure the memorable moments and time together. We don' treasure the money we spent or the fancy places that we did or didn't go to. We will never forget the kid who got carsick along the winding mountain roads and just fifteen minutes from our destination, or the one in the backseat who puked five minutes after leaving to drive the twelve hours home, after just eating a huge donut.

Some of our best vacations are when we just sit with our family on the deck, eating great food and watching the kids have fun as they play with their cousins. Other vacations are jam-packed with activities and experiences that we can't do in our home state of Iowa.

While packing up in a hotel room, we've seen a pod of dolphins playing right from our room's window. We've run across a beach, as the sand kicked up behind us, to reach the water's edge before seeing them swim out to sea. We get another free dolphin show right in front of us and a few more minutes of watching surfers ride small waves. It's something that we don't get to see if we stay home.

Our trips include very long car rides to save money on airfares, staying with family in other states, eating lots of good food, and sightseeing. It's nothing special, but it's very memorable for all of us. Years later, we will still talk about those vacations and pull out thousands of photos.

There is one vacation we try to take every year. There were a few years when we weren't able to go: when I was nine months pregnant and this past 2020 year because of COVID-19. But it is a week that we don't like to miss. It is a fun-filled week at a big Bible camp on the lake. There are no TVs, there is poor Internet service, and there are lots and lots of great people to spend the week with. It's a week full of games, activities, family time, relaxing by the lake, rock climbing, zip-lining, bonfires with roasted marshmallows, and any type of tournament you could think of. There are soul-filling chapel services and friendships that will continue, even during the years we aren't together at camp.

I know that I sound like an advertisement for the camp. Well, there is a reason we make a point to spend a week vacationing there. It is so good for our souls, and our family gets to connect with other wonderful families. The bonus is no electronics for a full week. It's like an electronic detox for the whole family. And a revival for our soul.

One day, our kids will tell their children about their family vacations, just like we tell them about ours. It's about making memories that last and that make them want to share them with their kids. At family gatherings, we hope that they will talk about memories like the vacation when Jack almost broke his leg or the one when Mom got a tattoo.

I've never heard anyone coming back from vacation without a story to tell or a great memory from it. Even if the vacation was awful, there is still a story behind it.

"How was your vacation?"

"Oh, it blew. We got a flat tire, and we had to be towed to a town where everyone had the same last name. I was sick with food poisoning for three days. I spent the trip using the camper bathroom while we were driving down the interstate through a hurricane."

Okay, so only part of that story is true, and it's not even my story, but you get the point. It may not have been a vacation with good memories, but memories were still made during that dreadful vacation. There will forever be stories to tell.

If you don't take a break from everyday life, work, or even family, what stories and memories will you have to tell at holidays or pass down through the generations? There's the one about my grandpa always wanting to fly his small plane on family vacations to save time and my mom getting sick in the back every time. It's not my story, but when I see the picture of my grandparents, my mom, and her brother in front of that small plane, every single time, I think, Mom is about to get sick in that thing. I hope they remembered the puke bags."

It's not only important to take those family vacations but

also to get away with your spouse too, without kids. Recharge your relationship. It's just as important for you as a couple. When you come home refreshed and recharged, your kids will notice the difference that a few days away from them can do for your mood. You'll still have stories to tell them but only the clean ones.

When we came home from our one-and-only adult vacation in fifteen years, we told the kids that we had been attacked while we were in the ocean and that we had needed to go to a Mexican doctor's office. Their eyes grew to twice their size, and they wanted every awesome detail. We then had to confess that we had not been attacked in the ocean by an animal but that a tow cable had given us nasty cuts and scrapes.

It may be time for another grown-up vacation. We need some new stories. We can always use the chance to recharge our relationship and intentionally make time for each other for a few days. Now I'm going to spend hours online searching for the most beautiful, romantic, and budget-friendly place to visit. Then I will get around to planning and booking it in another three-to-five years. But I have to start somewhere.

If you don't take a break from work to make memories with your kids and spouse, they will remember that too.

NOTES FROM GRAM

What is the definition of *vacation*? It is going outside, taking deep breaths of fresh air, and walking one-sixteenth of a block down the sidewalk four times. That is my daily vacation. Let's call it my before-coffee vacation."

One of my regular favorites was Grandma camp. It started all the way back with my little grandkids in the 1980s. We took trips by wagon or on little trikes around the neighborhood, had backyard treasure hunts, ate pizza on a Friday lunch out with

Grandma and all her friends, fed the ducks and geese down at the river, and crossed that river on the swinging bridge (Yes, it really did sway, and some of those little grandkids would run across it a dozen times while one timid little one waited for Gram's steady hand and crossed that thing with her eyes closed tight).

Vacation should mean getting away. One year, we decided to return a day early, sneak into our home, and relax twenty-four whole hours before having to return to normal life. We opened the wine, ate frozen dinners, and neglect our phone messages. We were thankful that we didn't have a long day of travel still ahead of us. Until the time that our small-town mailman saw us pulling up and loudly hollered for all of the neighbors to hear, "I've got all your mail in my truck. Welcome home!" That ended our anonymous return.

For the first seven years of our marriage, my husband's only vacation was the obligation of National Guard Camp. That was before the phrase "separate vacations" was invented. Vacations deplete the bank account, except this one: I bunked in my old bedroom and let our children be spoiled by their grandparents.

I know there were wonderful moments with fantastic scenery, no alarm clocks, campfires, and s'mores. But I put those on the back shelf of my memory bank. On the first day of a six-week journey to Alaska, which we had been planning for a year following our thirty-fifth wedding anniversary, it could have turned into a very silent vacation.

We came to a needed rest stop so that my husband could get rid of the morning coffee. While he went, I decided that since we had stopped, I had best make use of the facilities also. I neglected to note that the keys were in the ignition, as I got out and locked the doors.

Thanks to the Canadian Mounted Police, they got a locksmith for us, and we were on our way again, just a few hours behind schedule. Thirty-five years of wedded bliss got us through the frustrating debacle. It was probably good that it hadn't happened on our honeymoon.

I'm enjoying thinking back on our vacations. I remember returning from Hawaii, opening the garage door, and finding a huge pile of snow inside on the garage floor as a welcome home gift. There was a conference at Tan-Tar-A Estates resort in Missouri, where we rented bikes on a free afternoon. On a rural country road, a bull snake was crossing the road. I slammed on my brakes, and my husband ran smack into me. I added crutches to my wardrobe for a month. I'm reminded of that trip every day now, as I hobble on that arthritic knee.

The definition of *vacation* has changed for me. I'm in my eightieth decade now. This means that in the summertime, I go to my deck and watch the traffic. In the winter, I head to my heated porch to make sure the young folks are still going to work on time. My journeys this week are two blocks to the beauty shop and one mile to the hospital for my yearly mammogram. I guess that I won't be bringing back any souvenirs from any grand adventures anymore. But I will toast all of those moments with a glass of wine, per my doctor's prescription.

Surviving a Global Pandemic

*Y*es, I'm totally serious. It's July of 2020, and during the last four months, we have been living through a global health crisis. Never in my life, did I think that I would be writing a chapter like this, much less using the word *pandemic*. I had to google it when it first started. We wake up each morning and hope that today, we are headed back in the direction of what normal life used to be.

If you were raising children in 2020, I'm sure you remember the coronavirus well. If you were a child in 2020, pick up a history book. (Even Google Docs no longer spell-checks coronavirus because it has become such a commonly used word).

In the United States, the COVID-19 virus spread first in Washington state, way back in January of 2020. By March, the virus had made its way to the Midwest.

During spring break, we learned that it was too risky for kids to go back to school and that until further notice, they would be learning from home, or schooling at home as we called it. Using Google classroom and Zoom, the kids went through three months of learning this way. Some days were much easier than others were.

But it is far from over. School is set to start in one month, and we still have no idea what it will look like: home, in the classroom, wearing masks, or not wearing masks? There are no instructions on ways to handle this crisis. There are no rules, no guidelines, and little information about the virus. So political leaders and world health organizations are making up the rules and changing them as we go. Information changes daily: symptoms, risks, what works, and what doesn't work.

Words like *quarantine* and *COVID* are used daily in normal conversation. Social distancing and wearing masks are how we interact with each other.

Big birthday celebrations are a thing of the past. Instead, people drive down the street, honking and waving signs that say, "Happy Birthday," and head on their way without cake or games because we can't risk getting sick.

We live in fear of a cough. A handshake and hug spread much more fear than love and joy. The test for COVID-19 is a nasal swab that has been described by adults as, "Horrific," and, "I'm pretty sure they cultured my frontal lobe." So when my three-year-old had to be tested one night at the urgent care, I cried tears of guilt, as she lay very still and behaved better than any adult having their brain swabbed. As an essential worker, if her tests came back positive, it would be my fault. There is no greater guilt a parent can carry than that of getting your child sick.

We don't know if our kids will or even should return to school this fall. Sports are canceled. State fairs and concerts are canceled. Playgrounds and swimming pools are closed. Movie theaters and restaurants are empty. We order our groceries online and pick them up. Even cat food and toilet paper from Target is ordered online and picked up. There is a nationwide shortage of toilet paper, cleaning supplies, medical gloves, surgical masks, and thermometers. The only beer left on store shelves is Corona.

There is also a shortage of bicycles, trampolines, swimming pools, board games, chalk, and construction paper. This means that our communities are finding new things to do with their little families while isolating. At a time when you would think that internet usage would be at an all-time high because everyone is stuck at home, it hasn't been. People are enjoying their time together, riding bikes, making creations with chalk to brighten social media fields with the photos of smiling children making their neighborhoods beautiful, swimming in their own pools, and even baking together. For several weeks, I couldn't find sugar and other simple baking supplies at the store.

During this time of isolation we have bought a trampoline

and created new things with Legos, construction paper, chalk, pillows, and blankets. The kids even learned to make banana bread (clearly a staple in our home).

Life has changed more than any of us could have ever imagined, but one thing is certain, isolation has brought us together, as a family, community, and world because we are all in it together, and it's not over yet. We have accepted, adapted, and changed for the good and health of our families and communities.

Wearing masks and taking our temperatures is a normal part of life now. Talking with friends with six feet between us is normal. Ordering food to go instead of eating out is normal. Facetime and Zoom girls' nights are normal instead of gathering in person. But, man, I can't wait for the day when I can hug my parents and siblings again. That will be a hug that will never be taken for granted.

In the midst of this pandemic we celebrated our fifteenth wedding anniversary—a big one. A year ago, we had talked about celebrating it on the beach in Destin, Florida. An adults-only vacation to the beach for this big anniversary had been our plan for a while.

Then flights were grounded, state borders were closed, and Florida quickly became one of the COVID-19 hot spots. So the big anniversary trip was never booked. As July 16, 2020, approached, we talked many times about just celebrating later in the year when we hopefully would be allowed to travel. I was already scheduled to work that day and all that weekend. It looked like it was going to be just another normal day, that is, until I pulled into the garage at 9:15 p.m. on our anniversary.

I was greeted by my two dashing boys, who were dressed up. They handed me a towel and my robe and told me that I had to go straight to the bathroom. There I found a hot bath sprinkled with rose petals and the room lit with countless tea-light candles. As I sunk into the hot water, I grabbed the card that had been left for me. The pages were filled with fifteen wonderful memories of our life together. The last one read, "Join me on the deck."

In my bathrobe and with wet feet, I tiptoed to the deck, where I found more candles lighting a path to my handsome man sitting there with more roses, candles, and cheesecake. I thought, *He hasn't been this romantic since we were dating, and he's still mine.*

When I sat down in a deck chair next to him, I was grinning from ear to ear. He had made our day so special. With our busy schedules and all that is going on in the world preventing us from a big celebration, it was unexpected. But celebrating our anniversary in isolation was perfect. Even the stars sparkled for us, and that's not just the romance talking. A comet was set to cross the sky at 9:45 p.m., just for us. Ha!

It was an anniversary celebrated during a pandemic. It was a romantic memory set in the middle of a global health crisis. We were making the best of this incredible life.

We don't have to change as the world changes around us. We can choose to wake up each day, ready to make a difference, sparking change, and being thankful for just waking up. The world and this health crisis don't have to change or define us. If we let God work in and through us, we get to decide what circumstances will change us.

Pandemic does not have to be a scary word. To me, it means something different: a change. I choose to make the most of things that life is throwing at us.

Let It Change You

Awful things will happen to you in life like living through a global pandemic. We are all going to face trials, heartaches, and possible devastation. Those things are going to break or make us. We have to choose which one it will be. Those moments, trials, and hardships might not be fair and may leave us with many unanswered questions.

They will inevitably change us. You can choose to become hard and bitter or use those moments to transform and grow. Don't just let them define you. Let them become you, giving you strength and courage. As the old saying goes, "If it doesn't kill you, it'll make you stronger." Well, I'm not ready to die. So, I'm the strongest I've ever been.

Some have lost loved ones, children, and spouses. Some have spent years being abused or raped. Others just always seem to have bad luck, never get ahead, or have a bad hand dealt to them over and over. Whatever it is, we've all had stuff happen to us. There have been and will be storms in your life. After one storm, we hope that we will be prepared for the next one.

Well, I had my defining moment. It's the trauma that made me who I am now: a strong woman who can raise good children, work forty-plus hours a week on second shift, write a book, and live fully. I have perfected the don't-mess-with-me stare, and I am ready when someone starts to cross my family or me.

I have not had to face many challenges in life, and they have not been to the extent of what many, many others have experienced. But the one that took the most from me also gave me most of who I am now.

Nearly fourteen years ago, I was dozing next to my first newborn. It was very early in the morning hours. That early morning feeding was done, and we were both resting peacefully next to each other in my big bed. At that time of day, my husband was working third shift, so he was still at work. In that early morning hour, I heard a commotion at the back door. My first thought was that it was Josh and that he was coming home from work.

I still thought this as I heard my bedroom door open. As a tired mom of a newborn, all I could think in that moment was to pretend that I was still asleep. I thought, *I don't have the energy right now to entertain my husband. I'm a sleep-deprived, new mom, and it's way too early.*

But just as I was thinking this, the bedroom door closed again. At this point, I felt a little slighted. Sure I didn't want to engage in any early morning conversation, but I didn't want to be completely ignored either. So, I thought, *I'll give him a few minutes to put his lunch away and brush his teeth. Then he should be coming to bed.*

Ten minutes later, he still wasn't back in the bedroom. That's when I decided to find him and find out the reason that he hadn't come to bed. But he was nowhere to be found in the house.

I then did what any slighted wife would do. I called him. I was ready to accuse him of ignoring me and leaving. When he answered the phone, I said, "Why did you leave this morning? Are you mad at me?"

He said, "What are you talking about? I haven't been home yet."

That's when I got really upset. I wondered why he would lie to me about something like that. "Yes, you were. I heard you. You came into the bedroom, and then you left. Why?"

"No, really, I haven't left work yet."

I thought, *What?* That's when it hit me. If he hadn't been there, someone else had been there. I hadn't heard that person leave. I wondered, *Are they still in the house? If they came into my room already, will they come back? Will they hurt me or my baby?*

I was finally awake enough to realize that someone had broken into my home. That person had come into my bedroom while I had been sleeping. I didn't know if they were still in my house. After the call to my husband, I called the police. I sat in my bed next to my five-week-old infant. I had no weapons to protect me, and I had nothing to make me feel safe. All I could do was sit between the door and my baby. I was ready to protect my child with my own life, if the intruder came back into my room.

The next thing I heard was my husband. I have never heard him scream like that before. He came screaming and running into the bedroom with fear in his eyes. He had grabbed an autographed baseball bat from our display case on the way in the house. He came in through the busted back door. He didn't know what he was going to find when he got to us. Neither of us was knew if the house was empty or not.

Shortly after he arrived, the police arrived too. They found us in our bedroom. Josh was armed with a prized baseball bat. I was on the bed with my newborn sleeping right behind me. They searched our entire house, and they didn't find an intruder. Thankfully, it seemed that the person who had broken in had stolen my purse and run out without taking or disrupting anything else,

There was $1,000 worth of damage to our back door. I had lost one credit card, debit card, some cash, two social security cards, and the secure-digital camera card that had all of the photos we had taken at the hospital when our first son was born. But we had our lives. Everything else was replaceable.

As I tell this story, you may be thinking, *What's the big deal? You didn't even know someone was in your house until that person was already gone.* That's true, but I think that's the blessing of it.

A few months after the event, the police were able to catch and arrest our intruder. We not only learned who he was but that he was a registered sex offender.

He had left me alone. At first I joked, "I must not have been his type." Sarcasm was my coping mechanism. I realized that if I hadn't thought it was my husband coming home from work and had seen the person entering my home—his face with its sharp cheekbones and piercing eyes—I didn't know what he would have done. I thought, *Was he armed? Would he have let me live if I had seen his face? Would he have raped me or god forbid, my baby?*

Those thoughts consumed me for months. I spent two weeks sleeping at my parents' house. Then I spent another three months sleeping on my couch with my baby in a Pack 'n Play right next to me. When my husband was able to get a first-shift position, I started to feel safer in my house. But it was no longer a home. That was for sure. The intruder had taken that away from me. It was a house. It had four walls and rooms that no longer felt safe in the daylight or the darkness.

It hardened me. I trusted no one. I still don't. But years after this trauma, I know that it has shaped and defined me into a stronger version of myself. I went from thinking, *But what if someone breaks in again?* to, *Go ahead and try, You won't be leaving in one piece.* Whether it was actually true or not didn't really matter, as long as I believed it and it got me through the night.

As I said before, months after the intrusion, they caught the guy. He was a forty-five-year-old registered sex offender, with kids of his own. I was asked to give a victim's statement at his sentencing. He didn't even have a trial because the evidence that was found at his apartment was enough to forego a trial. He admitted his guilt, and he was sent to sentencing.

This has been one of the hardest things that I have had to do. I had to face the person who violated my peace, home, and life. That day came, and I entered the courtroom dressed in a white button-up shirt and wool dress pants. I remember exactly what I was wearing that day, how my hair was done, and what the judge looked like. But I remember nothing else. Because facing my intruder was too much for me. He entered the courtroom, and from that moment on, I could look at no one else but the judge. I would lose it if I looked at the man who had changed my life.

When I was asked to give my statement, I stood up, shaking. I read from a paper that I had worked on until it felt that it said exactly what I was feeling toward this person. I spoke every word while my voice shook and looked directly at the judge. He had dark hair, glasses, and he was maybe forty or fifty years old. I knew his face wouldn't show any reaction to my words, but I felt like I saw a hint of sorrow or fear, as I spoke them. I was speaking toward the judge, but my words were for the man who had violated my home. He was sitting in the opposite corner of that courtroom.

I finished my shaky statement, and after wiping away tears for the tenth time, I sat down. That's when I heard a snicker from the other side of the room. My head immediately jerked in that direction before I realized that I was looking at the man for the very first time. My blood was boiling. I wondered why he had laughed after I had just stood up in front of him. The last few minutes had been the most difficult ones of my life. That's when things changed for me. A switch flipped. I didn't care about him anymore. I cared about *me*: how I felt, my life, and my children.

I remember my intruder's name, his hair color, and that he was slightly balding. I remember the color of his eyes look, his age, and that he lived close to the home that he had entered—mine. I don't know if I can ever forgive him for what he did. But I can definitely thank him for who I have become because of what he did to me.

I am who I am because of what I have been through. I love the woman I have become. I do not apologize for being that person. I may be too much for some people, and maybe I can't offer enough kindness and sympathy to others because of it. But I am who God has made because of the things that I have lived through.

It's terrible to have to go through hard stuff in life. I am not trying to minimize the things that others have been through. Believe me. I know it could have been so much worse. Because it wasn't worse, I truly believe that I had an angel looking out for me that day. A registered sex offender broke through the glass of my back door, unlocked a dead bolt, walked through my home during daylight hours, came into my bedroom, saw me sleeping next to my newborn, and walked out with only my purse. Yes, I totally know it could have been *so* much worse and life ending. Thankfully and by the grace of God, it wasn't. So I'm using it to change me into a better version of myself.

Am I still scared? Yes. Do I let fear control me anymore? No. I look it dead in the eyes, grab it by the shoulders, and say, *Try me. You're not going to get through me without a fight!*

Work, Work, Work

*W*hat do you want to do when you grow up? Why do we always ask young people that question?

Do we ever really know the answer to that question?

At one point my heartfelt answer was, "I want to be a juvenile court judge so that I can help children in trouble." Of course, I would still like to do that, but after a year of studying prelaw courses in college, I realized that it was not the path for me.

Look, I love my job now. I help people every day. That was always my goal and the thing that I was good at. If you were to ask me what I want to do when I grow up, my answer would be, "I want to help people. I want to write. I want to retire in a lakeside, mountain cabin. I want to spend time with my family."

We need to keep asking ourselves what we want to do when we grow up because the answer will always be different and we are still growing up. After twenty years of job experiences, three college degrees, and one rewarding career, my answer to the famous question would be different today than it would have been a year ago.

I have been a nanny and waited tables. I worked as a secretary at a radio station and a private school, as a professional photographer for several years, and in law enforcement. Now I am working in a rewarding career as a diagnostic medical sonographer. In English, that means ultrasound tech.

Most days, I love what I do. Of course like any job, we all have those days when we want to throw in the towel and walk out. But there is something rewarding about what I do. It makes me keep walking through that hospital door each day. Most days, it's the appreciative smile from my patient because I'm helping solve the problem that the individual was having or to why that person hasn't been feeling well. I might be giving that individual the best news of his or her life, such as she is finally pregnant after years of trying or numerous failed attempts.

There are also days that make me question the reason that I keep doing it and days that break me. I find a cancerous tumor in an otherwise healthy person. A smiling couple comes to see their unborn baby on my screen, and the baby no longer has a heartbeat. I can't tell them what I see. My patient is dying, and the only thing that I can do to help is remove fluid from his or her body so that this person will be more comfortable.

On those days, I shed a few tears after my patients have walked out of the door. I say a silent prayer for them and for God to work because I know in my heart that He still has a plan. That is why I will come right back the next day to do it again. God is working, and I am helping.

Some days are just plain harsh. They drag me over the coals. Some days, I have to be brave, use my big-girl voice, and fight through the tough stuff. Some days, I am blessed to meet a patient who lights up my day, my week, or even the whole month.

I was not put on Earth by mistake, but I was put here to help people. I will continue to do that at work, at home, and in my community, no matter what job God calls me to do.

Grown-Up Birthdays

I just turned thirty-six. I'm no longer in the lower thirties. I am now in the higher thirties and closer to the forties. I'm at an age now when my husband thinks it's funny to say on my birthday, "Aren't you forty today or at least older than me now?" Then he walks away laughing. No; it has always been no. It's not funny when you've just climbed over to the dark side of thirty.

What do birthdays look like at this age? Well, the day before, I started the prep work. I started at 5:30 a.m., after sleeping five hours and getting ready for all the appointments that I had scheduled for my day off. I went to three school conferences, bright and early. After leaving my toddler with a babysitter, I went to a waxing appointment to have hairs violently ripped from my body, just to feel younger and smoother when sitting around the pool. I ran errands, and I dodged phone calls from political campaigners and scammers. I had a hair appointment in the afternoon, which was the first opportunity that I had to sit down and relax that day.

While in the salon chair for two hours and behind a face mask, I chatted with the lovely twenty-year-old stylist. During the first few months of the coronavirus lockdown, salons were closed, and we all had the COVID cut or color. Either we were brave enough to cut or color our own hair at home or we let it grow long and wild with grown-out roots. We waited and longed for the salon doors to open again.

When they finally did open, it took weeks to get an appointment, and face masks were required for service. Sitting for two hours with foil on my head, a mask on my face, and a cape around my neck quickly became hot and claustrophobic. But it felt good to finally interact with the sweet young stylist, who was in training, as she touched up my roots.

Because I was a busy mom who was going to appointments, running errands, and planning a birthday girl's nighttime get-together, I ran out of that salon with dripping-wet hair. I did not have enough time for my stylist to blow it dry. I told her that I was sure that it would be perfect and promised to send her pictures of the finished work, when it was fully dry.

I ran more errands. I picked up the following week's groceries. Then I met the lucky woman to whom I had sold my espresso machine. I hear you gasping. I know. I sold my espresso maker. But that's only because it was taking up space on my counter next to my other espresso maker, cold-brew carafe, and coffee maker. It wasn't the Keurig Rivo's fault that it wasn't getting used enough. It was time for it to go to a better family, which would show it the love and appreciation that it deserved. Why didn't I make one last latte before saying goodbye? Oh, the caffeinated memories we had together.

I headed home to put groceries away and prep for the evening that I had been looking forward to all week. Everything during the week had been leading up to this one evening. It was going to be a joint birthday celebration for me and three of my best friends. Our personalities were so different from each other, yet they were amazing women and very important to me for different reasons.

We loaded up our vehicle with snacks, beverages, bug spray, swimsuits, towels, and takeout and headed to my parents' house. Yep! The party was at Mom and Dad's house. Why was it there? It was held there because no kids or husbands were there. Plus, there were no rules or curfews. When you're in your thirties, it's fun to party at Mom and Dad's house.

We sat in the hot tub and near a bonfire. We listened to reggae party music and made silly mom-dance moves. Picture the movie *Moms' Night Out* and the Amy Poehler, Tina Fey comedy flick *Sisters* colliding into one incredibly fun girls' night, except that no children were lost and no property was damaged—that we know of. The only casualty was the poor possum that ran in between the tires of our moving mom-mobile. Things were said and done that will forever remain in the inner circle of girls' night.

This all took place the day before my actual birthday, which was also a lovely day of relaxing, having food made for me, and my laundry being done by someone else. I called the shots the entire day. After having to be reminded too many times that it is my day and that I got to decide what to do and eat all day, I frustrated my husband when I asked him again if there was anything that he wanted me to pick up for him while I was out getting the car washed.

He exclaimed, "Why do you do that? I can get your car washed and pick up whatever you want."

I wondered why I needed to explain to him that I was just trying to be considerate. I'm a mom. It's only mom-nature to think of family members' wants and needs above our own. What? Don't dads think like that? Okay, maybe that was a little harsh. He did a great job of making me feel loved, relaxed, and pampered on my day.

However at 12:01 a.m., my special day is over. I have to get up, take the toddler to the potty, and change her pajamas. I tuck her back into bed, after once again frantically searching for that tiny, ratty giraffe. Mom takes very limited breaks. Even on my birthday, I still want to be the one who comforts and tucks her back under the covers, with sweet whispers and little nose kisses. It made the end of my birthday sweet and magical.

As I look back at the entire weekend, I realize that it was a pretty great grown-up birthday. It ranks right up there with the Barbie birthday I had when I was six or the Ronald McDonald birthday that my sister had when she turned four or five. My parents threw us incredibly memorable birthday parties while we were growing up.

I learned, from the best, how to host a pretty memorable, grown-up birthday party for a group of amazing moms. Even adults and especially moms deserve to celebrate their milestones too. Every year that passes, every visible laugh line, crow's foot, dark circle, and gray hair documents our milestones and memories.

I'm Gonna Go There

*W*e are all just trying to do the best that we can, right? Each day, we have struggles and a failure or two. But the next day, we get up and try harder than we did the day before. We vow to do better and be a better parent, spouse, and employee.

But here is the problem: We were born sinners. We were born not knowing right from wrong or how the world worked. We have to learn to think for ourselves, do what we believe is right, and be good people. Many of us learn these things from families, teachers, religions, books, and maybe even governments.

I've always been what I believe to have been a pretty good person. But maybe that is just an idea that I created for myself. I know that I'm opening a can of worms. But just hear me out for a few minutes.

It's currently 2020. Any of you who are reading this book shortly after 2020 will get what we went through that year.

SHORT RECAP OF 2020
(A Huge Election Year)

- The incumbent is Donald Trump.
- The year started off with a global pandemic that hit the US in January. It led to parents homeschooling their kids

and hundreds of businesses being shut down and closing their doors. Many people have been in total isolation for months. The COVID-19 virus continues to spread, and it has not tapered off as we head into the end of the year.

- Have you ever run out of toilet paper and Lysol cleaner? Well in 2020, it happens all the time. You have to hit up three stores, right after semi-trucks come with deliveries, to get a package of TP.
- There was talk of murder hornets.
- There is a racial war going on. Protests and rioting are happening in our cities every night.
- Police forces are being defunded and schools are too.
- There is apparently a coin shortage. I'm not sure how that one is possible. Maybe people are throwing their change into a wishing well and wishing for 2020 to be over already.
- Meetings, school classes, birthday parties, and end of life care are all held over Zoom video calls.
- A category-4 hurricane that blew through Iowa. Yes, a real inland hurricane called a derecho blew through Iowa! (It's wild because that is my home state, and we have *never* had anything like this happen before). The news neglected to report on it for a week because it was not the typical storm that happened in a flyover state.
- With that being said, there was an actual hurricane called Laura that reached a category-5 when it hit land in August.
- It is required to wear a mask when entering any public establishment. Many businesses are closed. Sports are canceled. We are all twiddling our thumbs and wondering what we are going to watch on TV this fall.

It is now September. It has been a whirlwind year and the craziest that any of us have ever experienced.

While I approach this chapter with caution, I also know that anyone who is reading and remembers this year can totally relate and will likely be nodding along silently saying, *Yas, girl* (Don't ask. I have no idea how or when yes turned into yas, but it had to be sometime in 2020).

In a political year that could completely divide a nation, it hasn't … yet. I believe it hasn't broken us yet, despite its trying hard because we are a nation of individuals who would rather befriend their neighbors than live in a divided community separated by hate due to our differences. We are no longer a nation that believes every issue is black or white or right or wrong. We believe that we can talk about best practices and solutions for a current situation. We are a nation of strong people who refuse to fail. You can hit us with all you have—and trust me the political parties have sure tried—but we will prevail. In the end, you will find us all standing together in unity.

We are a nation that is more like-minded than two separate political parties. We are a nation that when we sit down for coffee with a neighbor who may vote differently than we do, we realize that our views on important matters of the heart are much more aligned than a two-party system would lead us to believe is possible. This is how a two-party system fails us every time.

Despite the 2020 political war going on, this is what most of us have learned during our difficult year: We agree that we love people, regardless of race, gender, or occupation. We want to help pick up the pieces of a community that has been destroyed and left in mounds of debris and families who have been left with no home, no food, and no electricity. Even when we are required to social distance, our hearts still reach out to these families. We step into their shoes, and we would give the clothes off our backs and food in our fridges to help them make it through another day of devastation cleanup.

We want to be there for loved ones when they are sick. Nothing else matters but family when you can't be with family members during their last days. ICUs are filled with sick and dying loved ones who have no visitors due to COVID-19 health restrictions.

While all of this is going on around us, the political campaign is still going on in the background. However, there are less people watching the news and getting drawn in by the hostile campaigns. This year, we are focusing on getting things back to normal and not who will control the next four years because *we will.*

If anything, it has taught us that we can't be controlled by a party. We will prevail, no matter what storm we face. We will unite despite the person that we check off on the election ballot. Will there be a winner and a loser? Yes. But after surviving 2020, that person will answer to us—the strongest, most-united nation under the sun.

We will proudly wear T-shirts that read, "We survived 2020." Oh yeah, we did. On the other side of it, you'll find me stronger than ever, telling my president what to do and not the other way around.

What Do You Do when You Don't Know What to Do?

I've shared stories of what not to do. I've told you about some of my mistakes and the lessons that I've learned, hoping it will reach at least one of you. Maybe it will prevent the same mistakes, embarrassments, and tough stuff that I've gone through.

But what do you when you just don't know what to do? I don't know. I don't have an answer or a solution at this time.

What do you do when you are at work, have a busy schedule, are short staffed, and then get a call from school telling you that you have a sick child and a call from daycare saying that your little one is bleeding from her nose? Yeah. I didn't know what to do either. I left the one at school lying in the office. The one with the nosebleed fell asleep for a long nap at daycare. I stayed at work. I was so busy that I didn't even have time for a dinner break. I only called about the kids once. Talk about major mom guilt not knowing the right thing to do.

But I did it. I had to make decisions on the spot, even though I didn't know what the right one was. Everyone survived, and with a good night's sleep, those decisions that I made didn't matter the next day.

Usually when I don't know what to do, I pray and then ask

my husband. It's a good habit to always pray first, whether it is a big decision or a little one and whether you know what to do or don't know. In those moments when you just don't know what the answer is, pray hard. Then go ask your husband or Mom (Usually, she's another good one for advice) what to do.

Depending on how much time I have before I need to make a decision, it usually looks like this. I have a momentary, internal meltdown, maybe cry a little bit, pray fast and hard, call Mom or text your husband, focus, put all the things together in my head and heart, and make that decision with confidence ... hopefully. The next time you face that situation, you'll know if it was the right call or not. We are always living and learning.

So how about this? You do what feels right in your mama heart. Don't worry about what others will do and say or the advice that you will be thrown. What feels right in your gut for you and your family is exactly what you should do. Instead of trying to be the best mom, let it go to the One who has it all and allow Him to do it for you.

Still Surviving a
Global Pandemic

𝓘'm still trying to make the most of this pandemic. At the beginning of this year, who knew that by this point, it would be normal to wash face masks with your delicates and to have a hook full of them next to the car keys so that you could grab one every time you left the house.

But here we are. It's now been twelve years. Oh, wait. I'm wrong. It's been nine months. But to all of us working on the front lines of this pandemic in a COVID hot spot, it sure feels like it has been twelve years. We've only made it this far because of sarcastic humor and funny 2020 memes. They are my life. I can't get through a quarantine day without sending and receiving a few of those hilarious gems.

There is no dress code because we aren't going anywhere. Do I want to wear the same sweatpants for days? It's no problem. I don't want to wear a bra? It's no big deal because no one is around to notice. The 2020 fashion trend is cozy and comfy. It doesn't matter if you've been wearing the same thing for days. It's only a Zoom meeting. No one knows that you are business on top and slob on bottom.

We made it through the summer. COVID's infection rate began to decline, so we all let down our guards. We are still in the middle of it. Tomorrow is Thanksgiving. Our infection rates are skyrocketing. Then Thanksgiving is canceled. Who knew that a national holiday could actually be canceled? When hospitals are overcrowded, ER wait times are in the hours, nurses and doctors haven't rested for days, and every other patient I do an ultrasound on is positive for COVID-19, then yes, holidays are indeed canceled.

You could say that this is the worst holiday season ever. But just wait. A completely isolated Christmas might be on its way.

We've already spent birthdays in quarantine. This means that there are no birthday hugs or spankings, for that matter, from grandparents or erratic aunts. Now it's Thanksgiving, a holiday that millions spend surrounded by extended family. Christmas is quickly approaching. As Michael Buble croons, "I'll be home for Christmas," from my tiny Bluetooth speaker, the thought that crosses my mind is, *Not this year, Michael Buble, not this year. Keep Grandma healthy and your butt at home.* This is followed by a sad chuckle because it's true.

While this year may be the worst holiday season that I have ever seen in my lifetime, it is not the worst the world has ever seen. We are isolated, people are sick and dying, and many have lost their businesses and livelihoods during statewide shutdowns. Yet it doesn't compare with the holidays celebrated during the world wars. Families were torn apart by war, and people died from famine. The years in between world wars were spent battling the Spanish-flu pandemic. So while we may have our worst holiday season this year, it is not the worst in history. For that, I count all my blessings, from the quarantine of my little home.

We will still cook the turkeys, even if we have to eat the entire bird alone. We will throw green-bean casseroles in the oven. Nana has shipped out homemade cheesecakes so that we will have a little taste of home on Thanksgiving Thursday. We may be celebrating small and isolated, but we will still follow our traditions.

Morning will still start with the Macy's Thanksgiving Day Parade, but there are no crowds of smiling spectators this year. Parade floats are filled with costumed people wearing masks. These are not costume masks either, but they are surgical and fabric masks that cover the nose and mouth and protect and prevent illness and infection.

Some families are celebrating on the curb. Some are picking up Thanksgiving dinner from Mom's driveway. The food has come straight from Mom's kitchen, and then it is taken home to eat alone so that Mom will be safe and isolated. Other families are sharing the responsibilities and the food but are eating it in separate houses. Whole turkeys are cooked for only three people.

How long will this global pandemic last? No one has any idea. We are in the second wave of it for sure. It's possibly the third, depending on which scientists, graphs, or models that you look at. COVID's numbers keep spiking. The hospitals aren't slowing or quieting down, as weeks go on with this virus.

Slow and quiet are two words that are *never* uttered in a hospital, and just typing them will probably bring wrath upon my place of work. This is especially true because it is a full-moon weekend. People who work in health care or as a public servant are superstitious of a full moon.

Instead of spending Black Friday in long lines and touching elbows with hundreds of people, we will shop online from our couches. Forget ever touching a stranger in the near future. There will be no handshakes, hugs, or even fist bumps. A public sneeze warrants worried glances from anyone nearby. Every time we step out of our homes, we have to think, *Do I have a mask with me?*

In 2019, if I had seen someone wearing a mask over her mouth, I would have thought, "My, I wonder what illness or cancer she is battling." In 2020, someone who isn't wearing a mask can be fined by the police. I know that it's unbelievable. I hope that by the time you are reading this, things have changed, and we are no longer walking around sporting masks. My favorite mask, which is in my purse at all times, has the words, "Coughy filter," right across the mouth of it. We have found masks to accessorize or match our outfits. If we must wear them all the time, we might as well have fun with them.

I'm trying to have a positive attitude. I'm trying not to write these chapters negatively. After all these months, it's hard to find positivity, even deep within me. I hate reading in the news that our depression rates in the US have reached one-third of the population. That's one out of every three people. That's just the number of those who are seeking treatment or just admitting it. Okay, that's enough of all that.

I do have a good story to tell. Today was the first time that I had a COVID patient recover. She spent more than a month in the hospital's ICU. She even spent a few days on a ventilator. She was so sick from the coronavirus that a machine had to breathe for her. This is a pretty common occurrence with this illness.

Miraculously, she survived being on the ventilator, and after a few days, she was able to come off of it. But her struggles from the virus were far from over. When she regained consciousness, her doctors and therapists discovered that she had developed "COVID brain," a term used for someone who has suffered so much from the virus attacking the brain that she cannot speak, walk, or do much of anything physically. Some people who have suffered this have not yet recovered from it. Doctors don't know if they ever will. But my patient did.

With extensive therapies, she is now able to speak. She can have full conversations with people. She can walk without assistance. This is a huge milestone for someone who was recently unable to even breathe on her own. When I had met her, she had been in the hospital for just over a month. She told me that she was finally going to be released in the next two days. She wouldn't be home in time for Thanksgiving. Now as I'm writing this, I realize that she was released today.

I asked her what she was going to do first when she got home. She said her first priority was hugging her grandson. Because she had had the virus and had recovered, she was no longer a risk to her family—at least not while she still had the antibodies in her. So she had planned to wrap him up in a big hug. She had missed him so much.

I was so thrilled to hear her story of how far she had come

to recover that I started to cry. She looked worried, and I said to her, "Don't worry. These are tears of happiness. They are the first I have had in many months. You see that in health care, we don't see many recoveries. We are dealing with the sickest of the sick, and many don't make it. It's very wearing, both physically and emotionally.

"But sitting here with you and hearing your story is exactly why we keep coming into work every day, even when it feels like it's too much for us to do. You are why we continue to have hope, help, and expose ourselves to this virus every day. Please go tell everyone you know of your story."

She cried, and I cried. Then she promised me that she would write down every detail of her journey through COVID, from her first symptom, to her recovery, and to going home. I told her that one day soon, I hoped to be lucky enough to read it.

It may sound silly to you as you read this. Maybe the world is far into the future now, there is a tried-and-true vaccine for COVID, and there is no longer a constant fear of the virus. But now while we are in the highest peak of this second wave, hearing these stories of recovery and writing out my thoughts and emotions on this page are what keep me going. They are the things that give me hope that next year, the holidays will be much better.

One day soon, we will be able to hug our family members, have backyard barbeques, and sit with friends and neighbors long into the evening hours on a summer night. I'll kiss those little nieces and nephews that I haven't seen in such a long time. I'll even feel comfortable shopping inside Target and grabbing a Starbucks in person, instead of always ordering online and through a busy drive through. Oh, the things that we take for granted. I tell you that I will never do it again.

This weekend, I came across this song on Facebook. So far, I have listened to it about one hundred times and have only bawled to the point of having puffy, red, and squinty eyes a dozen times. Here is a little backstory about the song so that you can google it and cry your eyes out too.

It is a song by Alicia Keys. More than a dozen beautiful children sing the cover song like the angels in heaven. It was sung as a tribute to COVID-19 heroes and all of the past, present, and future mommas out there. She wanted them to know that they are doing not only a good job but also a fantastic job. I know that it doesn't get said enough, so I am telling you right now, look up the song, cry hard and long because it really does help. Know that beyond a shadow of a doubt, you are amazing, and you are doing a good job.

> I see your light in the dark
> Smile on my face when we all know it's hard
> There's no way to ever pay you back
> Bless your heart, know I love you for that
> Honest and selfless (selfless)
> The world needs you now
> Know that you matter, matter, matter
> —Alicia Keys, "Good Job," accompanied by One Voice
> Children's Choir

NOTES FROM GRAM

There are years, and then there are *years*. I thought this September would be magic when I turned eight-eight on the third day of the month. I passed my driver's test, except I'm not driving anywhere. At least, it is good for two years.

Guess what? I am not bored. I'm perhaps a bit more still and arthritic, which I blame on not getting in and out of the car. So what if I am slow?

As the day disappears, I look back and check if I accomplished the one chore I assigned myself that morning. Usually, it is checked off, but if not and with God's will, I always have tomorrow.

Ten years ago, we downsized and moved to a condo on the river. I recommend this move to all widows who need to change their habits. Widowhood brings more time: no planning menus, less laundry, no watching boring TV games (except for the Iowa Hawkeyes and Cyclones that is), and no sharing the daily newspaper. The river doesn't seem bothered at all about the world around it.

With all those thoughts about how the world has changed this year, how do I tolerate a pandemic when aloneness is already given? There are advantages to isolation.

1. I haven't filled my car's gas tank in ten months.
2. The grocery deliveryman is, "Glad to do it," instead of, "Who does this old lady think she is?"
3. For a while, I often had coffee with a friend as we sat six feet apart in the garage. But winter has arrived, and now we converse by computer.

I admit that life is much different in the COVID era. But my parents were scared that I would get polio. No doubt, my grandparents experienced the 1918 flu scare. There were no antibiotics in the foreseeable future back then. I was a nursing student who cared for iron-lung patients, but I was never ill during the toughest of times.

Each generation is better off because life throws a few events our way to wake us up, to make us feel blessed to have beautiful sunrises and full moons, and to know that we are not the one in charge.

What Kind of Ponytail Do You Want Today?

$\mathcal{T}$he biggest daily decision for a four-year-old girl is what kind of ponytail she wants to have that day. Or maybe it's a braid day instead.

It has been a different world raising a toddler girl than it was raising toddler boys. Most days, Lord, help us. The neighbors probably think that I am beating my daughter with her hairbrush rather than gently brushing through the tangles.

My sweet little girl has the most beautiful curls in her light brown hair, which is naturally highlighted with streaks of blonde. Her soft, silky, and shiny curls are what women spend a fortune over a lifetime to obtain. She was blessed with these envious locks, and we aren't even sure where it came from. My hair is fine, dark (naturally), and paper straight. My husband's hair is thick and a little bit wavy, but it is definitely not curly.

Taking care of her hair every morning is no small task. She knows that it has to be done each day to prevent the nightmare that will ensue if we have to brush through a day's worth of wild, curly tangles. The job is easiest when I do it right after her bath and those beautiful, long curls of hers have been conditioned, and they are still wet.

Then a process begins. I have to get her thinking about it by asking her what she wants done that day. Preparing her reduces the risk of the epic tantrum. I lay out the supplies: brush, tangle spray, hair tie, and matching bow. I also need my phone, not for Pinterest inspiration or how-to videos but as a bribe.

Yep, I'm not above bribing in certain circumstances. Hair combing is one of them. The compromise is that she gets to play on my phone while she sits nicely on the floor, and I braid or put her hair in a ponytail. I know. I've been manipulated by a four-year-old, but if you could only hear her screams when there is no distraction. I'm just waiting for DHS to show up at my door.

She has become so clever about it that she will bring me her brush, tell me to braid her hair, and then ask for my phone so that she can play for a few minutes. Neither of us will argue about it because we are both getting what we want. I get soft untangled hair that is pulled back and out of my toddler's sticky face. She gets to play the Elmo game while I tightly French braid two little rows on her head.

When did kids learn to negotiate at such a young age? I think parenting has evolved from a parent saying, "You will do as I say because I said so," to a parent saying, "Okay, here are your two options. You need to pick one of them." Personally, I don't think that there is anything wrong with either way of parenting. But the latter seems to be a bit more effective these days. The best part is that I can still choose those two options.

The world gives us choices for everything in life. So I guess it just makes sense to parent our children in the same way. In the twenty-first century, everything we do is a choice. No one tells us, "Do this because I said so." If someone does say that, we know that we can turn around and walk away. I believe that it is a very different world than the one our grandparents grew up in.

In our house the most effective results come when we offer choices. Our kids feel that they have options and independence when getting to choose. It's a win-win for me when I choose the options.

As a child, the rule was that if you wanted to keep your hair long, then you had to

A. Keep it out of your eyes.
B. Brush it every day and do something with it.

My sister's solution was cutting her hair. My solution was bottles and bottles of Johnson's No More Tangles spray, brushes, hair ties, braids, and topsy tails. Do you remember those? It was a simple little ponytail turned upside down and inside out. When my daughter asks for those, we call it Jasmine hair because just like Aladdin's Princess Jasmine, we can rock a few topsy tails.

We also have the Elsa or Anna braids and Belle hair. To a four year old, it makes deciding so much more fun when you get a hairstyle like a Disney princess.

The life of a toddler isn't that tough, especially when the only decision you have to make for the day is one braid or two. I pray that for many years it is the hardest decision she will have to face. I hope that this harsh world will not get to her innocence and make her decisions tough.

Why is it different raising little girls than it is raising little boys? It's not always that different. She plays with her brother's action figures—for a moment—before playing with her ponies and dress-up clothes in the next.

The way that we teach and shield them from the tough things is very different. With my delicate, gentle little girl, I want to cuddle, hug, and protect her from seeing the ugliness of the world. With our boys, we educate and inform them with long thought-provoking conversations, which is followed by their very good questions.

It's not that we don't hug and cuddle with them too because we do, especially when all of their friends are looking. We are those parents who will deliberately embarrass their children in front of all of their friends. It's a good thing that they don't seem to mind and that they usually just respond with a quick hug, a shy smile, and reddening cheeks, which makes their adorable dimples pop.

But whether it is right, wrong, or because they are older and more mature, it is still different. For as long I can, I want to protect their innocence and them from seeing how hard life can be.

When I can't shield them from it anymore, I want to teach them how things can be different, how we can make a difference, and how we can be a light in dark places. Sometimes all it takes to make someone's day or the world better is being kind, smiling, showing respect, lending a hand, hugging someone, loving each other, and giving unconditionally. It's about living for God every day.

If that is all my children ever learn from me, I will have succeeded as their mom. Just those few things will brighten the world each day and turn ugliness into something beautiful. Maybe I'll teach them how to do a topsy tail or a couple of French braids too.

The Teenager

One day not long ago, my oldest asked me for a pain reliever for his headache. I walked into the kitchen and pulled out two pill bottles as he sat down at the counter with his head in his hands. I shook out two white pills for myself from one bottle and two white pills for him from another bottle. I told him where his pills were on the counter, and then I turned around to fill my cup with water. I noticed as I walked back to the counter to take my pills that they were no longer there. I asked my very smart thirteen-year-old if he had taken my pills instead of his own.

"No. I took the white ones that were sitting right there."

"Those were mine. Drew, you just took my Midol."

Mortified, he shrieked, "Ah, what's going to happen to me?"

After teasing him a bit and telling him that it would help with his period cramps, I silently prayed that it would help with his angsty teen emotions. Briefly, I thought about crushing some up and adding it to his dinner occasionally.

I was once a teenager and not an easy one at that. But I was definitely not expecting the emotions and outbursts from a teenage boy. Thankfully, his outbursts are fewer and farther between than my own teenage tantrums were many years ago. I had them daily and even hourly on some days. Those teenage-girl hormones were so unpredictable.

My sweet firstborn child has a heart of gold. He is tender,

kind, respectful, and thoughtful. For a thirteen-year-old, it is remarkable that he will consider other people's feelings before his own. We hit the kid jackpot with that one. He is a rule follower, and he would do anything for his little brother and sister. With such a glowing personality, I'm not even sure that he's mine. Besides him looking exactly like me in photographs as a child, I would have worried that he was switched with another baby at the hospital.

As proud parents of three amazing children, all we want for them is to feel loved, find joy in life, and follow God. This kid wears it daily. Whether his face shines with love and joy, or he puts it on as protective armor in our unpredictable world, there is no denying that he is praying and seeking God daily. Because he is the oldest child and biggest role model to his younger siblings, it is my prayer that as the younger ones get older, they will look up to him and model his behavior and heart.

Raising children is hard. Raising a teen is an entirely different challenge. It's like walking into a jungle and knowing there are dangers out there but not knowing what or where they are. It's having your guard up at all times because one of those dangers could strike out of nowhere and at any time.

That's what it feels like raising teens in the twenty-first century in our agitated, divided society. Threats and dangers are around every corner, in the classrooms, on our councils, and right outside our front doors. All of the sudden, our children hit that age when they think that they know everything, want independence, and are smart about social dangers. I think, *Um, excuse me. You are still a child. Back up and take a seat.*

When exactly does that happen? I remember those days as a teen when I was fighting tooth and nail for my independence. I believed that my mom and dad were clueless about the tough things that I was going through and that they did not understanding how hard life was. Now I'm the one being told,

"You just don't get it, Mom." No wonder my parents looked at me with a hint of amusement in their eyes and chuckled. Now I'm the one looking at my teenage son the same way.

Yet I remember crying and crying with real heartbroken feelings because, "No one understands me. No one gets it." Oh, if I could only go back and roll my eyes at teenage me and tell her that yes, as parents, we get it. One day, I hope my son will look back and realize that when he was frustrated and shouting, "No one ever listens to me!" that, yes, I was listening the whole time.

If one day, he reads this chapter and says, "I don't remember doing that." I will prove to him that he did it. I will show him that I have written it all down in a little book, complete with the date and time.

Waiting

*O*h, here comes the topic that I have avoided thus far. I still haven't decided if this chapter will be included. Earlier chapters have been filled with sarcasm, opinions, politics, and faith, yet I'm unsure about including this one. After you read through this chapter, just remember that I am the same person that I was at the beginning of this book. The same sarcastic, caffeine-addicted mom, who isn't going to judge your choices and mistakes. Because this is a safe space, and I am a friend.

Okay, here it goes. I was a virgin on my wedding day, and remarkably for our day and age, he was too.

Why was I scared to say that? Why am I scared of judgement because of it? Maybe it's because when someone has found out in the past, that person's voice and demeanor changed toward me. Either someone would make a face that said what he or she was thinking, or I would get follow-up questions.

You might not believe me. That's okay. You don't have to. But it's still true either way. So let me first humor you with some of the questions that I got when I revealed this information.

"You really didn't live together before you were married? How did you know it was going to work?"

No, we really didn't live together beforehand. In fact, I had a curfew up until the day before I was married. Seriously, how do you know it's going to work even if you live together first? I still can't guarantee it will last another forty-to-fifty years, but I have hope that it will. Let me tell you that statistically, couples who marry young and didn't live together before marriage have a higher marriage success rate than those who lived together or married later in life. That's usually when I want to insert a big mic drop or boom! But respectfully, I don't.

My future years of marriage are not guaranteed. It is something that we have to work at, just as hard as anyone else does. Believe me; I have made mistakes over the years that would end other marriages. I try hard, I'm committed, and I pray over our marriage. That's it. There's no magic answer.

"Well, how did you know he was the one then?"

Um, are you serious? Are you equating a life full of happiness and joy with the one to the things that he's packing and can bring to the table?

I don't have a more dignified answer to this. I still can't believe this one. Yes, I actually got asked this question.

Among other questions I've received, usually people just react with:

> "Wow, that's awesome."
> "I don't know anyone who does that anymore."
> "Good for you. There's no way that I could do that."
> "Oh, well you don't want to know about my history then."

I'm going to be completely honest and tell you that it was very difficult to abstain, especially when we knew it was not the popular thing to do. We knew plenty of people who were doing it. They wondered why we weren't when we knew we were going to get married anyway.

But I have never regretted my decision. It makes me feel special and loved knowing that he made the same decision that

I did, well before I was in the picture. As a jealous human being, I don't know how my heart or my mind would handle not being the one and only.

Look, I don't care what your decisions were. You will not receive judgement from me about your history. I care about mine and my convictions. I did it for me, him, and our children. Yes, I did it for my children. I may have high standards and expectations for them, but I could never expect something of them that I didn't do myself.

One day, if they make a different choice than we did, it is what it is. We have shared the reason for our decision with them. As long as they are safe, smart, and in committed relationships, what more can I ask for? We will love our children no matter what.

When You Realize that It's the Last One

*A*ll of the baby stuff slowly disappeared. Even while we were getting rid of it, I wondered just a little bit if we would ever need it again.

But now our youngest child is four years old, and I'm calling myself old. When people ask us if we will have another one, I use the excuse: "Nah, I'm too old, too tired, and too broke." I just don't remember when it actually became true.

Now that it really is the end of my childbearing era, I am looking back on those baby days and thinking, *Do I remember tucking her into her crib for the last time before we moved her into her big-girl bed and took that crib down forever. No, I can't remember it.*

When was the last time I cuddled her tiny, warm body and rocked her to sleep in the corner rocker, before transferring her to her crib? Nap after nap, book after book, and gentle rock after rock. Day after day, it was such a normal routine. Now the rocker is sitting unused in the guest room, and I can't remember the last time I rocked my baby to sleep in it, as she lay heavily against my chest.

I remember the headache of taking that old crib down. It was the one that had cradled all three babies over a span of ten years. We tried to convert it into a big bed with no instructions or conversion kit from the company, which had gone out of business years earlier. I remember fitting my random Amazon-bought parts together and finally constructing the bed. Then I tucked her in for her very first night in a big bed.

My baby was gone, and my toddler was born that night. It was also one of the few nights that she stayed and slept in her own bed all night. That first night, I don't think that I slept a wink. I lay on my side in bed staring at the baby monitor and watching her tiny body slumbering in a big bed. I had also done this when she had been a tiny baby sleeping all the way across the house in her own room and in a big crib.

At some point in the four years since she came quickly into the world, we have silently realized that she would be it. In the beginning, we discussed five children. Then during the years between the first two, as I struggled to get pregnant and experienced a very early loss, two was okay. Two was good and comfortable. But I think deep down in the depths of my heart, I knew it wouldn't only be two.

Years later, our only daughter came unexpectedly. She has completed us and become everything that we never knew we needed in our family. She has two adoring older brothers and a proud daddy wrapped around her tiny little finger. She has softened all of my sharp ridged edges. Just as the first two changed us, she is what God knew we needed.

The day she came into the world, we were all head over heels in love with her. She slept silently as she was passed from one family member to the next. Her tiny body was wrapped in layers of clothes and soft blankets. As she was placed in her oldest brother's arms for the first time, he was struck silent, and he wouldn't look away from her.

The rest of us in the room were chatting about her and her arrival, and we didn't notice that his were eyes squeezed shut and tears were falling from them onto his tiny new sister. We all panicked because we thought that something had happened.

After a long minute, he finally whispered through his tears, "I prayed for a sister for two years, and now here she is." That's when the rest of us erupted in happy tears. She completed each one of us. I now have an eleven-by-fourteen-inch picture of that very moment on my wall so that I will remember it forever.

That is why we have children, whether they are unexpected, planned, prayed for, birthed ourselves, or rescued. No matter how it happens, children will teach us what pure joy and true love are. They will teach us patience … the hard way. They will teach us that things can be simple, life can (and should be) fun, and it is sometimes okay to cry over spilled milk, especially when that milk was meant for a crying newborn, and it took a great deal of work to produce.

Having children also comes with great heartache. Sometimes that heartache is immeasurable: a miscarriage, the loss of a child, or wanting desperately to bring a child into the world but not being able to do so. Our hearts will ache whenever our children are sad or hurt. They will ache when our children experience failures or trials. They will ache still when our children are grown, and they have their own losses and heartaches. Yet we will wake up each morning to love, teach, and treasure those little heartbreakers.

Even with heartache there is great, great joy in having and raising children. It is the joy that makes the heartaches bearable. It is the joy that makes the greatest memories, which we will treasure well into our old age and recount as we sit on our porches watching our grandkids play.

There are a hundred reasons that we tell ourselves not to have children or more children. Fear is one of the biggest reasons. We say that we are too old, tired, and broke. Yet we continue to do it. It must be because the sacrifices, the pain, and the love are most definitely worth it.

As I look up from my screen and see only one of my little ones, who is begging to stay up ten more minutes, I think that I have all that I could have ever imagined.

Some days, they cause me to fly my white flag and surrender to all the chaos. Some days, I want just ten more minutes with them to soak up the cuddles and hugs that they give me. Some days, I see how big they have gotten and think, *I'm in a new chapter with them.* It's one that includes sleepovers, youth-group parties, less frequent hugs, inside jokes with friends, less cuddles with mom, more time at school functions, and less time at home. But my love will be constant, and I will be right here whenever they need me.

So when exactly did we decide that baby chapter was done? I really don't know. Some days when I'm scrolling through social media and I see a tiny, squishy newborn, I find myself wondering, *Maybe one more?* But then I look up and see the new chapter that I'm in. It's scary, just like having a newborn. But it's also exciting. I see the young independent people that we are raising. Proud doesn't even begin to describe what it feels like when I look into their ever-growing and changing faces. Somedays having a teenager is a little bit like having a newborn.

You Are Enough

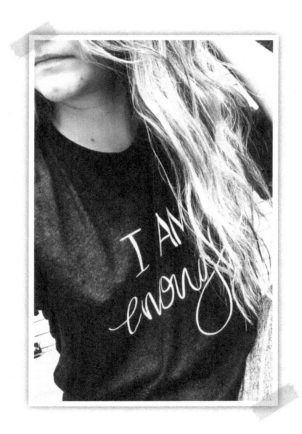

I am enough, and you are most definitely enough. You are everything, and you have what it takes to be someone else's everything. You have all that you need to be great. You are perfectly made. You don't need anyone to tell you who or what to be.

I know that you are wiped and feel like you're failing. I get it. You are going from sunup to sundown, and you feel like you're drowning. I know you don't need sympathy because you'd do it anyway. There is no glory, and there is no reward. You'd do it anyway.

It is enough. You are enough. Everything you do is enough. You are remarkable.

As I tell you these things, I am looking into the mirror and telling myself that I am enough. I'm enough, just as I am in my sweatpants and with my dirty, graying hair. I'm enough, even though those cookies for school were bought at the grocery store and not baked by my own hands. You know that the only person who is bothered by those things is me.

I'm tired. Can I just be tired without feeling guilty about all I have to do? I hurt, ache, fail, and cry. Kelly Clarkson is blasting through my speakers and reminding me, "I am broken. And it's beautiful."

It is because I am also strong. I am bold. I am phenomenal. I am enough.

I am enough to be saved by a loving God. I am enough to be loved by a wonderful husband. I am enough for my children, who need me. I am enough to be respected. I am enough to be a good friend. I am enough.

It doesn't mean that I don't need you. I do need you. I need your love, support, and friendship. But I don't need you if you want to change me, you don't accept the person I am, or I'm not enough for you. I surrender to God, and I will only change as He works in me.

My dear friend, if you remember nothing else of what you have read in these pages, remember this: You are wonderful. You are loved. You are needed. You are most definitely enough.

Keep working hard, loving fiercely, and letting God work in you. You mean so much to many people. Say it with me. I am enough. I am flawed and still worthy.

We Won't Live Forever

*T*his week, we experienced the loss of our family patriarch, my grandfather. We know these things will happen one day, yet we are never prepared for them when they come. When the news hit, I was in front of a computer at work with my back to my coworkers. Tears came hard and fast, and then the sobs started, right into that yellow paper mask over my face because of 2020. I knew that one day, this would happen, and I still wasn't prepared for it because how can you prepare?

Since then, the tears have come in waves, and the memories have as well. There are tears, laughter, more tears, and memories. Then the belly laughs come and bring more tears. I think about the funny little antics that made my grandfather the remarkable man that he was.

This is life—the full circle of it. Yet we do not expect and prepare for it. Instead, it hits us full on like a truck, a ton of bricks, or a crashing wave. Knowing that one day it will happen to us all doesn't prepare us for it when the end does come. But feeling all of those emotions full force at once confirms the wonderful life that was lived.

The only comfort comes from knowing that one day, we can be with them again. This is the assurance of heaven. Either we already know that it is where our eternal home is and that this earthly one is just temporary, or we hope in heaven and just need to step over that faith line into the assurance of a heavenly eternity. Either way, we can rest assured that we will be reunited with our family and loved ones. That hope helps me to heal.

Over the past couple of days, photo albums have been dug out. Hundreds of snapshots from little disposable cameras have been found at the bottom of boxes and dusted off. I touch each carefully and look at it for several moments, as I smile and have a flash of that memory. They are the memories that we share across the old dining-room table and that make us gasp, "Oh, I forgot about that!" We see the little mannerisms that made him who he was. We smile and chuckle every time one of us grandchildren do the exact same thing in the exact same way.

What do we do from here? How do we move on from this big loss? I don't know. But this week, it has helped to talk to family members, the ones who are grieving just the same as I am. It has helped to look at those photo books. It has felt good to remember the little things about who he was. When we share memories and stories, it has helped heal our hearts.

Going forward, we will call and check in with each other more frequently. We will never ignore another phone call from an aging parent or grandparent. We will be intentional about seeing each other more than at holidays. We will make more memories and take pictures together.

One day, it will be our children and grandchildren trying to heal from our loss. As they sit around the worn, old family table, they will share stories of how they remember us always carrying gum in our pockets or the way that we waved with two fingers and said, "Hello, hello, hello!" Okay, that one may only be my grandfather, but the memory of who he was will be shared forever.

Make sure you leave them with the stories. Take the pictures and be in them with the family. If you must take them with a disposable film camera, make sure to get them developed. This was the way that my grandfather always took pictures. I hope someone out there still develops the film.

Leave them wishing for more time but not regretting anything unsaid or undone. Say the things, be there for the events, and call your dad to check in. Email grandma, just because it will be the best part of her day. Who doesn't want to make their grandma's day? She will be so tickled by it that she will tell all of the church ladies about her sweet and thoughtful grandchild who sent her an email.

Healing is a process. It will take time. Being more involved and having a closer relationship might make it harder, but won't you regret it if you don't do it? You will wish you had. You don't want it to come too late.

'Twas the Week before Christmas

'Twas the week before Christmas, and all through the house,
The virus was shared, possibly even to a mouse.

With a sneeze and a sniffle, from one hand to the next,
"No, it can't be!" I told my husband in a text.

It just wouldn't be in keeping with this miserable 2020 year,
To celebrate Christmas alone, in quarantine, and with a lack of Christmas cheer.

But as I tuck in all the little faces on day eight of isolation,
I say a prayer and give thanks that I am the only one with symptoms on this occasion.

It doesn't matter what happens or what causes it. We will inevitably end up feeling Mom guilt at some point or another. For me, the worst feeling of Mom guilt came when I finally contracted COVID-19, ten months after it first hit the United States.

I was in denial. It first felt like it was only a winter head cold. I had a sneezing and running nose, just like any other December after the first snowfall.

But then the dizziness came, so the denial turned into, "Maybe this is something more." One call to employee health, and I was quickly at the express care getting a COVID test. Just twenty-six hours later, I had the results: positive.

Those results came in the middle of making dinner. The stove was on. There was a counter full of food to dish up for the family. That little notification ping on my phone alerted me to my new test result. I opened it quickly. The only thing my eyes could actually focus on was the words,

DETECTED

CORONAVIRUS SARS-COV-2-PCR

Detected...

I had contracted the virus. I was the first one in our immediate family and our extended family as well. I needed a minute—or forty-five minutes. I needed to be by myself for a bit so that I could sit curled up on the bathroom floor and just cry. I don't know why. We all expected this to happen eventually. Actually, I think we were all just a little surprised it hadn't come sooner with me working in health care.

So why was I so upset? It wasn't a death sentence, per se. In fact, most people just felt like they had a cold. But the media had instilled the fear of the virus in us all. And even with all of the proper measures taken to protect myself and my family, I had now contracted it. That feeling that I had was Mom guilt.

I had now exposed my family to the virus, so I needed a minute. With the guilt, the fear came. I thought, *What if it's not just a cold for us. What if one of us gets very, very ill from this?*

Whether it was COVID taking its toll on my body or the fear and anxiety of it all, I couldn't sleep for days.

I had been off work for fourteen days. The kids were out of school. My husband was off work. My youngest child stayed home from day care. All of this went on for four weeks and until none of us were contagious.

I spent days suffering from headaches, body aches, fatigue, and nausea. I never lost my sense of taste and smell or had a fever, which were the telltale signs of this thing. I was up one day and then down feeling miserable the next. I was able to clean the floors and play a game with my family in the morning, and then by lunchtime, I was achy and out of it again. The virus sent you on such a roller coaster of symptoms for days.

It was now day nine, and I had been feeling good—good enough that I hadn't needed multiple doses of pain reliever, and I had only taken a fifteen-minute nap. It all happened at Christmas.

Through all of the ups and downs, isolation, and roller coaster of emotions, I tried to keep things as normal as possible. Many Christmas movies were watched. Baking commenced while we were masked and following all proper PPE guidelines. We sang and danced to all of our favorite holiday tunes. Then I crashed with body aches and immense fatigue. It was a Christmas like none other before it. That much was for sure.

It was that way across the world. Some people were isolated, some were suffering physically from the virus, and some were suffering financially because of what it had done to our economy. Some families were missing loved ones who had died from COVID. Many were missing loved ones because they chose to stay away from family members to reduce their risk of spreading it to each other.

Weeks of isolation went on. People were completely alone. There were no Christmas or New Year's celebrations with friends and family. There were no coffee breaks or Target runs with best friends. There were no sledding excursions with friends from school or cousins and no living rooms filled with family, presents, and laughter. There were no kisses shared at midnight on New Year's Eve.

Yet it was one of the most enjoyable Christmases that I can remember. Our little family of five was nestled comfortably in our matching jammies, in our cozy living room, and around a beautifully lit Christmas tree. We enjoyed too much food, made new traditions, and spent weeks together with nowhere to go. We weren't ready for it to end when our isolation was over and we could venture out of our home.

No grandparents, aunts, uncles, or cousins, whom we missed dearly, came. But this Christmas in isolation taught us how blessed we were to have each other and how grateful we were that this sickness hadn't been worse for us. Worse things would happen in life. I was thankful and continued to sing praises that this difficult Christmas was not one of them.

Those few weeks together were some of the best in our entire fifteen years of marriage. There was something special about slowing down and focusing on each other. There were no other holiday commitments, parties, stress about finding five matching Christmas outfits for those parties, or Christmas Eve church services. We still enjoyed a service online from our living room, in our matching pajamas, and on this very laptop.

It was a Christmas that would go down in history. Next year, I hope to be surrounded by family and friends, who are healthy and joyously celebrating our year's blessings *together.* Together will be my word for 2021. After a year of quarantine and isolation, 2021, God willing, will be a year filled with family, friends, cookouts, reunions, parties, in-person church services, in-person school, holidays, and just overall togetherness.

So this year especially, I will raise a glass to good health. After a year like the one we have had, all I can ask for is continued blessings and gratefulness in my heart to carry me through this new year.

I haven't met one person who isn't ready to bid 2020 goodbye and jump feet first into the things that 2021 has in store for us all. May there be blessings, health, and goodwill to you all.

CHRISTMAS NOTES FROM GRAM

I have spent too much time over my coffee on this Wednesday.

Peace on Earth, goodwill to men.
But God, we must ask you when?
We wear our mask to avoid the air.
That mean old virus, we don't want to share.
The holidays are here but will soon be gone.
We hope and pray 2021 won't be so long.
But as I sit here with my coffee and contemplate,
Let's erase it all and clean the slate.
That means starting the year with a new attitude.
Clear your conscience and eat all new food,
A diet of love and understanding.
There will always be times that are challenging.
So tear off the ole calendar of 2020
And vow to see the new year with milk and honey.
Be grateful for every day you can rise.
Let sun or clouds or snow be a surprise.
Because we know as long as we live,
God's in control, and we can survive.
So happy holidays, friends, and to my clan,
Rejoice with grateful hearts. Amen.

Legacy

I wanted my grandmother to write this chapter. I wanted to read what she would say about legacy—leaving this world better than it was when you arrived, your family feeling loved and cherished by you, and your fingerprint on the hearts of every life that you have touched. She would pen such lovely and wise words on this topic. So I made sure to include her beautiful thoughts for you to contemplate on, right at the end of this chapter.

Do you ever wonder what people will say about you when you die? I know that it's a morbid thought, but after every funeral I have attended, I think about those things. How will people remember me? What will they say about me at my funeral? Will I leave a lasting impression on their lives?

Sometimes after a particularly beautiful funeral service, I shudder as I think those thoughts. Maybe they'll say, "Well, she yelled a lot," "She was a bit cynical and too sarcastic," or, "Did you ever notice her fingernails? Yikes." These and other awful possibilities flit across my mind.

Why do we think about these things? I think it's because we generally want to be good human beings and remembered for our good qualities, deeds, and services. Deep down, we really do care about what people think. We want to know that we mattered.

Our days have always been numbered. From our first breath to our last, they have always been known to God. We have no guarantee of tomorrow. So how will you live? How do you want to be remembered? What would people say about you today, and do you want to change that?

When I think about these questions and the kind of legacy that I want to leave, I think back to my grandparents—my living one and the ones who have already passed away. I think about how much they loved their family, how they taught us to be good people, and how important hard work was, whether managing a business, working the farmland, or spending long hard hours as a nurse and a mother to her own children.

Why did I decide to write a chapter on dying and our legacies after we are gone? I really don't know the reason. This chapter has had a title for months. So I must have known deep down that I had something to say about it and that it was important. Eventually, I knew the words would come, although I wasn't sure how and when.

Losing my grandfather recently has definitely made me think about these things a lot more. I see my kids grow and know that the growing doesn't stop, no matter how much I want to bottle up time and keep them little and close forever. I witness and read about people still dying every day from COVID. This year alone has made me think about these things more than any other year. Time is fleeting. What do I want to leave behind? What do I want said about me when I'm gone? What do I want people to remember about me?

I want to be remembered for teaching my children how to be kind and loving, working hard, and giving them memories that they will treasure forever. I want people to remember that I gave back with love, with my God-given talents, and to all those who were in need.

Do I want to leave my children with financial security and

assets? Sure, I do. But I know that I don't have to or that it'll be okay if I'm not able to because I am teaching them to value life, love, and family. I'm teaching them that it will be okay if they have to work hard for their own financial security, just like we are working hard for them right now.

When my time comes to leave this earth, I want to feel assured that I did everything that I could for my children, gave them all the love that I had to give, and loved my husband with my whole heart. I have the assurance of heaven and everlasting life with Christ. When I leave this earth, I also want them to know that I did all that I could, helped all that I could, and loved all that I could. Until then, my job here is not done.

NOTES FROM GRAM

This is what an eight-eight-year-old wishes for her legacy. What does legacy mean? To be a perfect person is too much to ask. But there are a few ideas that will gain you points toward that goal.

 a. Never forget, "Do unto others as you would have them do unto you."
 b. Forget the traits you don't admire in people. You don't need to be best friends with everyone but only kind and tolerant of others.
 c. Remember your good attributes. When you do things you aren't proud of, don't do them again.
 d. Think before you speak so that it doesn't come out in an unkind, judgmental, and offensive way.
 e. Don't put off good deeds like a phone call, email, letter, or a Facebook comment.
 f. Be generous because you can't take it with you in the hereafter.

Your legacy to yourself is memories. I recall my nursing career. There were good and difficult days, but I am thankful that it was a career of giving and that it taught me how to do and be the same.

I hope my legacy as a young mother was that I was usually there to listen. Every mother could do better in that department.

Don't forget to look back. Remember friends who were there for you and are now gone. Remember those who are there for you now.

Be thankful for life's experiences. I remember moving to Minneapolis, my first city, or the shock of southern living in vibrant Mississippi. For example, I wasn't too keen about flying in small aircrafts, but Jan (my husband) loved it and chartered his own small airplane, so I tolerated it. Plus, that view from the sky was always pretty fantastic.

Everything I Could Ever Want

There are candles on my birthday cake, and everyone is waiting in anticipation for me to blow them out in one big breath. But what if I don't have anything to wish for? What if I already have everything I could ever want? The only thing left to wish for is that nothing will change at all.

I have a Savior who loves me and the assurance of a life in heaven. I have a loving and happy husband and happy and kind children. I have a beautiful home that fits us. I have two families who love and support me and amazing friends who always get me. I have a career that I love and that provides food in my fridge and pantry, an abundance of clothes in my closet, and an old vehicle that I love, which gets me from one place to the next. I have good health (for now).

I may have too many gray hairs to count or pull out and just as many weeds in my lawn. I never have enough in my bank account to call it an actual savings' account and have to scrimp for every big adult purchase. There is definitely rust on my big SUV that I love to drive and noticeable rips in my old comfy couch. But none of that really matters when you already have everything that you could ever want and that money can't buy.

I have joy. It's more than happiness. It's actual contentment. In life, it is so hard to come by these days. I know firsthand how fleeting it is. It's here one day, and poof, it's gone in the next because of one thing or another that life has thrown at you.

Soak it up while it's here. Enjoy the joy while you have it. Live in it before the next adult problem or crisis comes. *Don't miss out on that joy.*

Society will tell us every day that we can't be happy without *X, Y,* and *Z.* We can't possibly be happy without grand success in our careers. There is no happiness if we don't have a brand-new beautiful home that we won't be able to afford. But don't worry because all of your friends are going to wish that they had your house. Car salesmen say that there's no way we could actually be happy unless we have leased a brand-new vehicle that costs too much per month. But don't worry; it doesn't have any rust, and you look great driving it.

I hop onto Facebook, and within five minutes, I have seen a dozen ads for things that Facebook thinks I need to be happy: purses, natural caffeine drinks, dresses that I googled once, and face cream that erases wrinkles and gets rid of maskne (In 2020, that's the acne that we have suffered from while wearing masks all day, every day). There is so much unnecessary stuff that will never bring us real joy. But the world tries to convince us that it will do just that. So we buy and buy and buy, until there is too much stuff in our homes and closets and we are no more happy than we were before we had all these things.

Social media highlights the very best of our lives—the things and moments that are supposed to make us happy. But with the camera filters, specific angles, and highlight reels of our best moments in life, is it really real? Maybe those special moments are, but too much of life is fake— lighting, smiles, attention, and news.

I have been guilty of falling into that fake happiness time and time again. I have followed all the things that the world has told me would bring me happiness. I guarantee that I will fall down that spiraling tunnel again someday. I will get caught up again in the things that society tells me will bring me happiness. I will chase the dream, even though I already have it.

One day, I will question my marriage again and fight to hold it together, as we have always fought to do in the past. I will cry real tears over whether or not I am being the best mom that I can be for my children. Someday, I will again search for jobs in another state because I'm fed up with where I'm at and believe the lie that the grass is greener on the other side, instead of being content at the great company that I have served for many years.

My life, marriage, and kids are far from perfect. But for today, this week, this month, and this year, I have found true joy in those things. It is a God-given joy and the kind that He has always promised us. I have joy in the life that I have created, in my marriage, and in myself.

Isn't that what we are searching for? Isn't that why we follow others on Instagram, scroll through Facebook, Snapchat each other our greatest moments, buy every book that is written hoping to fill our souls? Aren't we just searching for joy and meaning?

Stop searching. Look inside yourself. You have the answers right in front of you. They are in the soft round faces of your little ones, the stressed-out, exhausted relationships that you hold onto so closely, and even the worn-out roof over your head, which is protecting and keeping you safe and dry.

Imagine the change that you could make in your own home if you discovered that you already have the means to have real joy in your life. Imagine the change it would bring and the happiness your family would experience. Is it worth it? I think so.

Find your joy. Fight to hold onto it as if the world is watching. Hold it close, treasure it, and fight to keep it because joy is fleeting. You deserve to have it in your life … always.

Love you, friend. Thanks for hanging on.